Published by Seidlitz Education
P.O. Box 166827
Irving, TX 75016
www.seidlitzeducation.com

For related titles and support materials visit www.seidlitzeducation.com.

6.20

Content Review and Practice Book for the Texas Educator Certification Program

154 English as a Second Language Supplemental

Third Edition
Revised and Expanded

Patricia Morales, Ed.D.
Educational Consultant

ELL SERVICES

Irving, TX

Formatting and Editing Gaspar Rodríguez and Pam Duncan

For more information or for study sessions contact:
Dr. Patricia Morales at pmorales@ellservices.org

Printed in the United States of America
Content Review and Practice Book – 154 ESL Supplement
ISBN **978-09894123-2-2**

Dedicated to all educators shaping the young minds of tomorrow…

When students' language, culture and experience are ignored or excluded in classroom interactions, students are immediately starting from a disadvantage. Everything they have learned about life and the world up to this point is being dismissed as irrelevant to school learning; there are few points of connection to curriculum materials or instruction and so students are expected to learn in an experiential vacuum. Students' silence and nonparticipation under these conditions have frequently been interpreted as lack of academic ability or effort, and teachers' interactions with students have reflected a pattern of low expectations which become self-fulfilling. –

Jim Cummins

Negotiating Identities: Education for Empowerment in a Diverse Society (1996), pp. 2-3

TABLE OF CONTENTS

Disclaimer

The purpose of this study book is to help **certified** teachers study the domains and competencies for the 154 English as a Second Language Supplemental Test. This workbook includes: research-based content materials, resources to review and study the ten (10) competencies included on the test, helpful links to related literature, terminologies, and practice multiple-choice questions to review as part of teachers' preparation for taking the test. The practical questions are developed based on the test framework, which is aligned to the corresponding test competencies.

TEST INFORMATION: ***Visit the Pearson Website at***

www.tx.nesinc.com

for test registration, preparation materials, and for the most up-to-date information.

- Each question in the test booklet is a multiple-choice question with four answer choices (A, B, C, or D). **Expect questions that might require more than one answer.**
- You have a total of **five (5)** hours to take the test
- Breaks during the test? YES! You can take an optional break during the test. Just raise your hand!

Computer-Administered Testing (CAT)

- **NEXT** after you answer a question
- **BACK** will take you to the previous question
- **HELP** will assistance with buttons
- **MARK** will place a check mark next to the question you want to review. Clicking on **MARK** again will remove the check mark
- **REVIEW** will be available at any time during the test and will display the review screen of marked questions.

Test Taking Strategies

- ✓ Familiarize yourself with the test domains and competencies.
- ✓ Review and study the content of this study guide! Answer the practice questions!
- ✓ Become familiar with the question formats. You may see the following multiple-choice questions: a) Single questions, b) questions with stimulus materials, c) clustered questions.
- ✓ Determine answers based on your teaching experience and subject knowledge. Avoid selecting answers based solely on your isolated personal experiences.
- ✓ Focus on conceptualization of each decision set. Do not assume information that is not provided.
- ✓ Read the question carefully and **look for clues and key words**: first step, initial strategy, individual, beginner, best, etc.
- ✓ Read for meaning, for conceptualization (comprehension).
- ✓ Review test competencies, themes and main concepts a day or so prior to the exam.
- ✓ Become familiar with the **test structure**. The actual test includes **80** multiple-choice questions (The test may contain questions that do not count toward the score.)
- ✓ Do not leave items blank. There is no penalty for incorrect answers.

Prepare in advance! Take practice tests several times. Spend time learning the content!

Test Framework for Field 154: English as a Second Language (ESL)

Each content area or domains (3) to be tested is defined by a set of competencies written to correspond to state curriculum guidelines/standards, curriculum materials, and research-based theoretical and applied second language acquisition issues.

Domain I - Language Concepts and Language Acquisition

Approximately 25% of the test

LINGUISTIC

Competencies:

- 001 -(**C**) CONCEPTS: The ESL teacher understands fundamental language concepts and knows the structures and conventions of the English language.
- 002- (**A**) ACQUISITION: The ESL teacher understands the processes of first-language (L1) and second language (L2) acquisition and uses this knowledge to promote students' language development in English.

Domain II – ESL Instruction and Assessment

Approximately 45% of the test

COGNITIVE

Competencies:

- 003- (**M**) METHODS: The ESL teacher understands ESL teaching methods and uses this knowledge to plan and implement effective, developmentally appropriate instruction.
- 004- (**C**) COMMUNICATION: The ESL teacher understands how to promote students' communicative language development in English.
- 005- (**L**) LITERACY: The ESL teacher understands how to promote students' literacy development in English.
- 006- (**C**) CONTENT: The ESL teacher understands how to promote students' content-area learning, academic-learning development, and achievement across the curriculum.
- 007- (**A**) ASSESSMENT: The ESL teacher understands formal and informal assessment procedures and instruments used in the ESL programs and uses assessment results to plan and adapt instruction.

Domain III - Foundations of ESL Education, Cultural Awareness, and Family and Community Involvement

Approximately 30% of the test   ***AFFECTIVE***
➢ 008- (**F**) FOUNDATION: The ESL teacher understands the foundations of ESL education and types of ESL programs.   ➢ 009-(**M**) MULTICULTURAL: The ESL teacher understands factors that affect ESL students' learning and implement strategies for creating an effective multicultural and multilingual learning environment.   ➢ 010- (**I**) INVOLVEMENT: The ESL teacher knows how to serve as an advocate for ESL students and facilitate family and community involvement in their education.

Source: 154 English as a Second Language Supplemental Preparation Manual
Texas Education Agency – www.texes.ets.org

DOMAIN I

LANGUAGE CONCEPTS AND LANGUAGE ACQUISITON

Competency 001

This content area to be tested is aligned to a set of competencies that correspond to state curriculum guideline standards, curriculum materials, and research-based theoretical and applied second language acquisition subjects.

001 -(C) CONCEPTS: The ESL teacher understands fundamental language concepts and knows the structures and conventions of the English language

The beginning ESL teacher:

A. Understands the nature of language and basic concepts of language systems (e.g., phonology, morphology, syntax, lexicon, semantics, discourse, pragmatics) and uses this understanding to facilitate student learning in the ESL classroom.

B. Knows the function and registers of language (e.g., social versus academic language) in English and uses the knowledge to develop and modify instructional materials, deliver instruction and promote ESL students' English-language proficiency.

C. Understands the interrelatedness of listening, speaking, reading, and writing and uses this understanding to develop ESL students' language proficiency.

D. Knows the structure of the English language (e.g., word formation, grammar, vocabulary, and syntax) and the patterns and conventions of written and spoken English and uses this knowledge to model and provide instruction to develop the foundation of English mechanics necessary to understand content-based instruction and accelerate learning of English in accordance with the English Language Proficiency Standards (ELPS).

Source: 154 English as a Second Language Supplemental Preparation Manual
Texas Education Agency – www.texes.ets.org

LANGUAGE CONCEPTS AND LANGUAGE ACQUISITON

Processes of L1 and L2 Acquisition, Development, and Application

Human language is characterized by creativity. Speakers of a language have access to a grammar— a mental system that allows them to form and interpret both familiar and novel utterances. The grammar governs the articulation, perception, and patterning of speech sounds; the formation of words and sentences; and the interpretation of utterances. All languages have grammars that are equal in their expressive capacity, and all speakers of a language have (subconscious) knowledge of its grammar. The existence of such linguistic systems in humans is the product of unique anatomical and cognitive organization not found in other species.

W. Grady, J. Archibal, M. Aronoff, &J. Rees-Miller p. 11 (2001)

Key Terms/Topics

Phonetics speech sounds

Phonology - study of speech sounds

Suprasegmentals melody, rhythm

Morphology study of words

Syntax rules that govern sentences

Semantics meaning

Pragmatics - social situations

Discourse, speaking

Lexicon Vocabulary

Registers (e.g., functions and use of social and academic language)

Language proficiency (listening, speaking, reading and writing)

Structure of language (e.g., word formation, grammar, sentence structure)

Patterns and conventions of language

Language competence (e.g., linguistic, social, communicative competence)

NOTES

Defining Language

Through our language, we communicate our reality to others, or language is the means by which our view of the world is passed on to others.

Whorf, Benjamin. cited by Brown D. p. 29, 1987

Language: The language phenomenon is complex so a precise definition of language is not easy to provide. We might characterize language as flexible, responsive, and changing constantly to meet the communication needs of its speakers. *Language is systematic and generative; it's a set of arbitrary vocal or visual symbols that have conventionalized meaning; it's used for communication; it operates in a speech community or culture; it's essentially human and has universal characteristics*

Source: Adapted from Douglas Brown, 1987.

Communicative Competence

Grammatical knowledge plus the ability to use that knowledge to develop meaningful utterances.

Linguistic/Communicative Competence: Speakers can produce and understand an unlimited number of familiar, unfamiliar, and/or novel utterances. They recognize that certain utterances are not acceptable and simply they do not belong to their language.
Grammar is known as the mental process that allows human beings to form and interpret the sounds, words, and sentences of their language.

Social Communicative Competence: According to Brown (1987), definitions on communicative competence carried out by Canale and Swain (1980) and later by Canale (1983), reflect on second language teaching. The authors subdivide the **Social Communicative Competence** into four categories:

1. **Grammatical Competence**: this aspect of communicative competence encompasses knowledge of ***lexical*** items and rules of ***morphology***, ***syntax***, ***semantics***, and ***phonology***.
2. **Discourse Competence**: This aspect is a complement of grammatical competence; it has to do with the ability the learner has to ***connect sentences*** in stretches of discourse and to form meaningful utterances.
3. **Socio-Linguistic Competence**: This aspect is the knowledge of ***socio-cultural rules*** of language and discourse. An understanding of the social context is required; roles of participants, the information they share, and the function of the interaction.
4. **Strategic Competence**: This aspect deals with all the ***non-verbal*** and ***verbal communication*** skills the learner uses to compensate for breakdowns due to insufficient competence or variables related to performance. In other words, this is the way learners use to manipulate language in order to communicate what they want.

CONNECTION

An English language learner has to combine **Grammatical Competence** with the knowledge of how to use grammatical structures ***appropriately*** in the second language.

Levels of Language/Components of a Grammar

Phonetics: The articulation and perception of speech sounds as physical objects, the study of how speech sounds are made and perceived (e.g., how are speech sounds made, measured, and registered?)

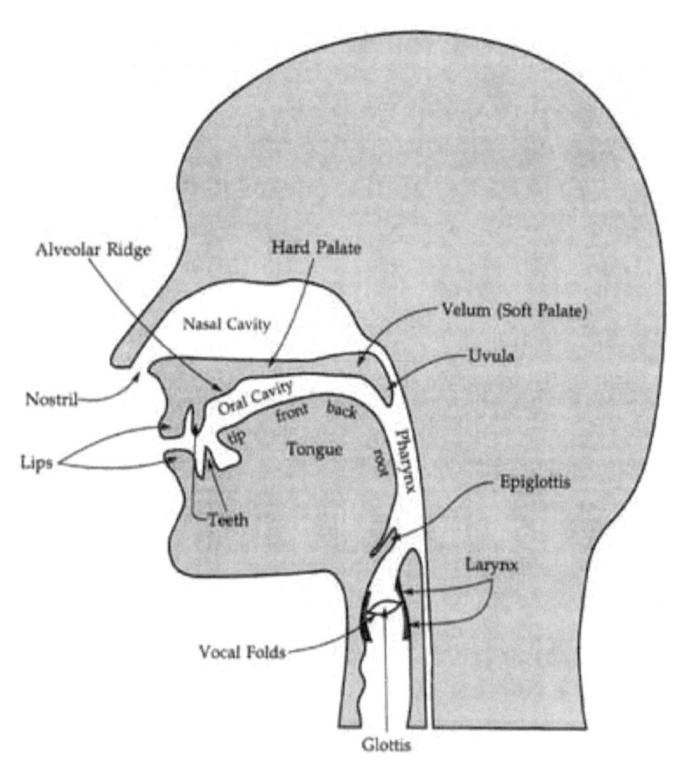

Dalbor B. J. (p. 24)

Speaking involves using the **active** and **passive** organs of the **vocal tract** (e.g., tongue, palate, alveolar ridge, velum, etc.) to shape and control the movement of the air that comes from the lungs.

ESL Reflection – Let's consider this:

- Human beings have basically the same active and passive organs in their vocal tracts and in their ears.
- Why are languages so different?

____
____
____
____
____
____

Point of Articulation: Where in the **vocal tract (mouth)** is the air flow obstructed? Lips, teeth, tongue, nose, velum, palate, alveolar ridge, etc.

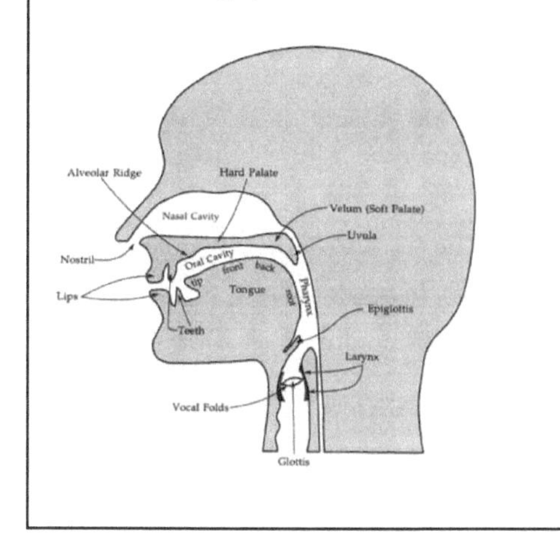

Manner of Articulation: To what degree is the air flow obstructed?

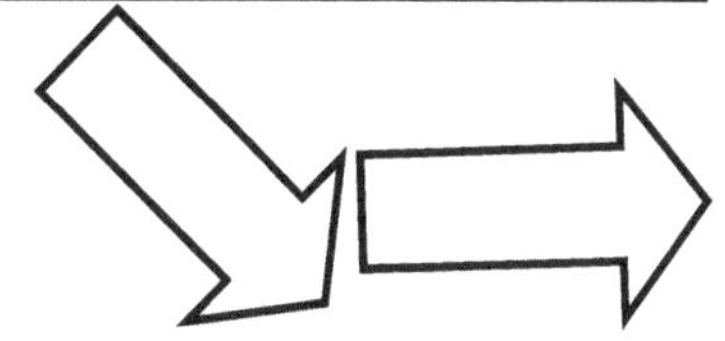

Examples In English

Stops (e.g., /p/, /t/, and /k/). The beginning sound in the words *pencil, take*, and *case*.
Fricatives (e.g., /s/, /z/, and /f/). The beginning sound in the words *sun*, *zoo*, and *fan*.
Affricates (e.g., /c/, /j/**.** The beginning sound in the words *church* and *Jim*.
Laterals and **medians** (e.g., /l/, /r/. The beginning sound in the words *light*, and *red*.
Semi vowels (e.g., the beginning sound in the words *yellow* and *well*.
Nasals (e.g., the beginning sounds in *man*, *nose*, and the final sound in *king, bank*, *sing*.

The table below shows the ***point of articulation*** and ***manner of articulation*** of some English sounds:

Consonants ***Phonemes*** in English

Point or Place of Articulation

Manner of Articulation	***Bilabial***	***Labio-dental***	***Interden tal***	***Alveolar***	***Palatal***	***Velar***	***Glottal***
Stops	/p/ pin /b/ bin			/t/ time /d/ dime		/k/ come /g/ gum	
Slit Fricative		/f/ fan /v/ van	/θ/ thin /δ/ then			/x/ who	/h/ hotel
Groove Fricatives				/s/ Sue /z/ zoo	/s/ shoe /z/ leisure		
Affricates					/c/ chin /j/ Jim		
Nasals	/m/ man			/n/ none		/η/ king	
Laterals				/l/ laugh			
Median				/r/ car			
Semi-vowels (Glides)	/w/ web				/y/ yes		(h) oh!

Source: Adapted from Stanley Whitley p. 16.

Phonology: The study of how a language organizes speech sounds into a meaningful system (e.g., How do languages organize sounds to distinguish different words?

Phonemes: Contrastive phonological units: The ***smallest units of meaningful sound***. They occur per the **point of articulation** (lips, tip of the tongue, teeth etc., and the **manner of articulation**: stops, fricatives, affricates, nasals, etc.). In English, there are, at least, 44 **phonemes** (sounds) and 26 **graphemes** (letters).

Vowel and consonant contrast examples:

ENGLISH

Vowel Contrasts	pin	bin	/pɪn/	/bɪn/
	bin	bean	/bɪn/	/bi:n/
Consonant Contrasts	pen	pan	/pɛn/	/pæn/
	zeal	seal	/zi:l/	/si:l/
	rot	lot	/rɒt/	/lɒt/
	hat	had	/hæt/	/hæd/

ESL CONNECTION

A phonemic instructional activity that focuses on targeted **minimal pairs** may help English language learners distinguish between different sounds in English.

Practice and usage of contrastive meaningful sounds (**phonemes**) in meaningful utterances is essential to improve word recognition, pronunciation,

Allophones: Members of the phonemes family. Allophones are sounds that occur in a phonetic ***environment*** (phonetic context in which a sound occurs); ***word-initial position***, ***word-final position***, ***word-middle position***, etc. Example: "Pam" /p/ in Pam is pronounced with aspiration (puff of air), becoming [p^h]

More Examples

In English, the consonant sound /k/ in ***kit*** is aspirated, [k^h], while the /k/ in *skill* is not

In Spanish, the consonant sound /b/in *abuela* is fricative, [β], while the /b/ in ***bicicleta*** is not.

*In the word **abuela**, the fricative [β], sounds like the phoneme /v/ in English; as in "vote"*

English Phoneme	**Allophone1**	**Allophone 2**
/p/	[p^h] in ***pin***	[p] in ***spin***

ESL CONNECTION

An English language learner at early stages of second language acquisition might sound out English words inaccurately by applying letter-sound association from his/her primary language (L1).
Spanish speaking beginning ELLs might pronounce the word "very" as /beri/, with a /b/ sound. This is called first language (L1) **phonological interference.**

Related Terms

Voicing: Voicing occurs when our vocal cords vibrate or not because of the pronunciation of the sounds. Sounds are called **voiceless** (unvoiced) when they do **NOT** make our vocal cords vibrate. Sounds are called **voiced** when the vocal cords **DO** vibrate.

In English, for example, **all** vowel sounds make our vocal cords vibrate. However there are certain consonants sounds that are voiceless.

The following examples share the same ***point of articulation*** and the same ***manner of articulation***, but they differ in ***voicing***:

Voiceless sounds: produced **without** vocal cords vibration. Put finger on your throat; you will NOT feel a vibration when sound is produced	**Voiced** sounds: produced **with** vocal cords vibration. Put finger on your throat; you will feel a vibration when sound is voiced.
/s/ as in Sue	/z/ as in zoo
/p/ as in Pam	/b/ as in bike
/t/ as in take	/d/ as in dime
/k/ as in come	/g/ as in gone
/f/ as in fan	/v/ as in van
/ʧ/ as in church	/ʤ/ as in Jane

ESL Reflection - ***Consider the questions below:***

STRESS OR EMPHASIS

Mary wrote a ***book?*** — Emphasis is on the object

Mary wrote a book***?*** — Emphasis is on the person

Mary ***wrote*** *a* ***book?*** — Emphasis is on the action or verb

INTONATION

Ask the questions below to a partner. Do the questions end up, down, or flat?

Would you like some coffee? *Would you like coffee or tea?*

Switch with Peter. Does the question end **up**, **down**, or **flat**?

Rising intonation' *Falling intonation*

Flat intonation

Suprasegmental Phonology (Prosody): Organization of sounds into larger units*:* ***length, tone, intonation, and stress.***

- **Length**: Duration of a sound; vowel/consonant. In English, long vowels as in "sheep" may take longer to articulate than short vowels as in "ship". In some languages, like Italian, some segments may differ in length alone. These long segments may be written with double symbol [nn] *nonno "*grandfather*" vs. nono "*ninth*"* In Tokyo, you want to be careful between ordering [bi:ru] "a beer" or [biru] "a building".

- **Tone**: The use of pitch (low pitch or high pitch) to convey meaning at the word level. Tone may be ***lexical***; it might change the meaning of the word. In some languages, like Chinese, the tone is ***lexical***: [*ma*] pronounced with high level pitch means "mother"; [*ma*] pronounced with low level pitch means "horse". In English; tone is not a factor whether you say the word "dog" with a high pitch or a low pitch, the word still refers to a pet.

- **Intonation**: Intonation distinguishes different kinds of sentences or phrases, and/or different words. Refers to the **rise** and **fall** of pitch over entire sentences. To convey surprise or irony, or to pose a question all languages use pitch pragmatically as intonation.

- **Stress**: A **prosodic** element used to give intensity or emphasis to certain syllables in a word, or to certain words in a phrase or a sentence. Stress may change the meaning of a word, both English and Spanish. See examples below:

English (**prosodic** stress)		**Spanish** (**prosodic** and **orthographic** stress)	
record	record	papa	papá
subject	subject	término	terminó

This phonological term is also used for similar patterns of phonetic projection inside syllables. Some languages, like Spanish, Cantonese, and Japanese are *syllable-timed languages*, so each syllable has roughly the same duration regardless of stress. English is a *stress-timed language*; some syllables are longer or more prominent than others. Syllables, in English, have internal structure; they can be divided into parts: **onset** or the beginning sounds of the syllable, preceding the **nucleus**, and **rime** (nucleus and coda).

ESL CONNECTION

English language learners might have difficulty distinguishing the meaning variation between sentences. ESL teachers should use effective concrete approaches to teach differences in speech, such as ***role play*** or ***acting out*** the sentences.

Morphology: The system of how words are built or word formation.

Morphemes: The smallest units of language that carry information about meaning or function. Morphemes **cannot** be divided in smaller parts. The word *books*, for example, has two morphemes "book" and "-s". "Book" is a root word or base word, and the "-s" is a suffix. A morpheme that can be a word by itself is called a **free morpheme** whereas a morpheme that must be attached to another element is known as a **bound morpheme**. For example, English speakers recognize that *cat* and *cats* are closely related- distinguished only by the plurality of the morpheme "-s", which is only found *bound* to nouns, and is never separate. English speakers recognize these relationships from their knowledge of the rules of word formation.

The morpheme *girl* is a free morpheme; plural *–s*, on the other hand, is bound. Complex words typically consist of a **root** morpheme (roots usually belong to a lexical category; nouns, verbs, prepositions, adjectives, etc.) and one or more **affixes** (bound morphemes).

Lexemes: Lexical categories that bear richer lexical meaning such as nouns (N), verbs (V), and Adjectives (A) and may serve as the roots for additional morphological variations.

Lexicon: The vocabulary of a language. Lexicon also refers to the total inventory of morphemes (**Free** and **Bound** Morphemes of a language).

Examples of Morphemes:

Unbreakable comprises **three** morphemes: - un (bound morpheme that means "not"; break- a free morpheme; and –able (a free morpheme that means "can be done")
Sailboat and **armchair** consist of two free morphemes. Sail and boat keep their original meaning but when they are together they form a new content word (free morpheme). The same happens with arm and chair, when they come together they form the word armchair.
Discussion consists of **two** morphemes: discuss- a free morpheme; and –ion a bound morpheme that results in a noun being formed.
Imperfections consists of **four** morphemes –im (a bound morpheme signifying "not"; -perfect- a free morpheme; -ion (a bound morpheme that results in a noun being formed; and –s (a bound morpheme that means plural).

Allomorphs: The variant forms of a morpheme (allomorphic variation). The morphemes used to express indefiniteness in English, for instance, has two forms —***a*** before a word that begins with a consonant and ***-an*** before a word that begins with a vowel, e.g., an orange, a building, an accent, a car, an eagle. The allomorphs of the plural morpheme for regular nouns: **-s** in cats; and –**es** in dishes.

ESL CONNECTION

Considering that not all languages attach prefixes or suffixes to a word root; repetition, practice, and check for understanding may be suitable techniques for ESL students.

Syntax: The system of how phrases and sentences are built from the words they contain, and how phrases are combined into larger phrases and sentences.

Syntax involves the order in which words are combined to create meaningful utterances, or sentences that make sense in any language. Languages use different syntactical patterns to form sentences into meaningful units of communication; spoken and written.

English language learners, while they go through the developmental process of English acquisition, transfer from their first language to English the grammatical structures (subject, verb, object, etc.) they recognize. Each developmental grammatical stage in second language acquisition requires that English learners apply knowledge from previous structures, as well as learn the unique grammatical structures in English.

ESL CONNECTION

English learners in early stages of English language acquisition might have ***syntactical*** interference from their first language (L1). For example, a native speaker of English knows how to combine or arrange the parts of a sentence to form a meaningful utterance, e.g.: ***I have a red car***; an English learner from Hispanic origin might arrange the parts of a sentence from the example given above, by imposing syntactical knowledge from Spanish e.g., ***I have a car red.***

English learners might misplace the position of grammatical categories of a sentence in English by applying ***syntactical rules and principles from their first language***. English learners require many opportunities to practice spoken and written meaningful sentences, utilizing effective learning strategies such as ***highlighting, underlying words, and cutting sentences apart (syntax surgery),*** etc.

Semantics: The study of meaning of words or the interpretation of words and sentences.

- **Denotation**: The meaning of a word in a dictionary; e.g., the denotation of the word "winter" corresponds to the season between the autumn and spring, regardless of whether it is cold and un-pleasant.
- **Connotation**: The meaning of a word in a certain situation. People give words different connotations using different ***prosodic*** elements; intonation, stress, pitch, etc. Pejorative or derogatory connotations are very common in some societies. For example, "housekeeper" and "servant" have the same denotation but different connotation. The word "servant" has a ***pejorative*** connotation in some societies.
- **Synonymy/Synonyms**: Are words or expressions that have the same meaning in some or all contexts, e.g., *purchase/buy, automobile/car, remember/recall; big/large.*

- **Antonym/Antonyms**: Are words and phrases that are opposite with respect to some component of their meanings; e.g., the meaning of *boy and girl* are opposite with respect to gender, although they are alike in other aspects, both belong to the category of humanity.
- **Polysemy**: This ***semantic*** relation occurs in situations in which a word has two or more related meanings; e.g., *bright = shining/intelligent; a deposit = minerals in the earth/money in the bank.* **A polyseme is a word or phrase with multiple meanings.**
- **Homophony:** This ***semantic*** relation exists in words in which a single form has two or more entirely distinct meanings; e.g., piece, peace; right, write.
- **Idiom:** A set of words or an expression whose meaning is not predictable from the usual meaning of the words. For example, "pulling my leg" (kidding), "it's raining cats and dogs" (pouring).

Pragmatics: The system of the use of language in social contexts; sociolinguistic awareness.

- **Discourse**: The connected series of utterances produced during a conversation, a story, a lecture, etc. Individual sentences commonly include elements whose interpretation relies on preceding utterances; e.g., *Mr. Pérez went to the beach. While there, he met a lady. Since, she was nice, he invited her for dinner.*
- **Discourse Analysis**: rules of conversation, speech registers, and nonverbal communication; Body language, gestures, eye contact, and physical distance are an important aspect of the social-communicative competence.
- **Register**: The way speakers use language in different styles depending on the context of a communicative event in terms of topic, audience, situation, experience, and purpose of the communication. Styles vary within an individual ***speaker's idiolect***; e.g., informal conversation with a friend versus formal interview for a job. Styles may be verbal and non-verbal. Differences in register can be conveyed in gestures, eye contact, and body language.

ESL CONNECTION

English language learners need many opportunities to use English language skills in social and academic setting. **Role playing** is an effective and concrete strategy to help English learners internalize social interactions, such as greeting or addressing different audiences, answering questions, and saying good bye.

Related Linguistic Functions

Language Borrowing: Words that we borrow from other languages: from Spanish, **sombrero** (from "sombra", meaning "shade"), **lasso** (from lazo), **hurricane** (from huracán, originally an indigenous Caribbean word), **chocolate** (originally xocolatl, from Nahuatl, an indigenous Mexican language), **barbecue** (from barbacoa, a word of Caribbean origin), **rodeo** (from the Spanish word rodeo).

Language Interference: ***Interf****erence* (influence) from the first or native language (negative transfer); e.g., A beginner, whose first language (L1) is Spanish might pronounce the utterance *I speak Spanish* as follows: *I espeak Espanish,* since Spanish does not allow 'st' blends in the initial position of a word. Language ***intra****ference* occurs inside the second language. An intermediate ELL may **overgeneralize** the "ed" suffix in "goed", "drawed", "comed".

Phonological differences: Different pronunciation (accent, allophones). The different accents that many English learners have are due to differences between the phonological system of their language and that of English. For example, a German might wrongly pronounce the English word 'while' as 'vile'. **Syntactical differences**: Differences in grammar use. English learners might misplace the position of grammatical categories of a sentence in English by applying syntactical rules and principles from their first language (L1). For example, a Spanish-speaking person might misplace the position of the adjective in "*Welcome to the* ***show big*** *ladies and gentlemen"*, causing a change in meaning.

Code-Switching: When a speaker alternates two or more languages in the same sentence (intra sentential) or between sentences (inter sentential). This ***interlanguage*** pattern occurs among ***beginners*** of a second language. To communicate, they alternate languages orally, and in writing. Code-switching is also the ***alternate*** use of ***two languages***; the creative use of communication by ***fluent bilinguals*** who know **both** linguistic codes. This use of two languages can occur at the word, phrase, clause, or sentence level. This is a very common situation when two languages are in contact; common in border cities such as Brownsville, McAllen, Rio Grande, etc. This kind of purposeful code-switching is considered a ***language phenomenon***.

Examples of Common Code Switching Patterns Among Fluent Bilinguals.

Pattern: Situational Switches Related to the social role of the speaker:
Example: Mother uses English to chat with her daughters but switches to Spanish to reprimand her son.
Pattern: Contextual Switches Situation, topic, setting, etc., linked to the other language.
Example: Students switch to English to discuss details of a math exam.
Pattern: Identity Markers In*-*group membership stressed.
Example: Ese bato, órale, ándale pues used in English conversation, regardless of actual Spanish fluency.

Source: P.16 of Valdés-Fallis, G. (1987). Languages in Education Series, No 4: Code-Switching and the Classroom Teacher. Arlington, VA: Center for Applied Linguistics.

ESL CONNECTION

A beginner ELL, may **insert** (orally and in writing) a word from his/her first language (L1) to communicate in English. The use of the first language by the English learner is also categorized as **code-switching**. English learners use vocabulary they are familiar with to communicate in English. For example, Pedro, a beginner ESL student from Guatemala might say: ***My name is Pedro. I go to Miami para vacaciones. Mi hermana is Mirella.***

Basic Conventions of English Grammar

ESL teachers' understanding of patterns and conventions of English language features such as word formation, grammar, vocabulary, sentence formation of spoken and written English will help them plan the way the subject matter is delivered. Instructional planning must include English Learners' language proficiency levels (beginning, intermediate, advanced, and advanced high), and their academic background and conceptual knowledge of the subject matter. The following is a list of examples and simple/basic definitions of English grammar rules and patterns.

Singular and Plural Nouns

A **noun** names a person, place, thing, or idea. For the plural form of most nouns, add '**s**'. For example: bottle – bottle**s**, cup – cup**s**, pencil – pencil**s**.
For nouns that end in 'ch', x, or 's' sounds, add **es**. For example: box – box**es,** watch – watch**es,** and fox-fox**es.**

For **nouns** ending in 'f' or 'fe', change '**f**' to' **v**' and add **es**. For example: wolf – wolv**es**, wife – wiv**es**, and leaf – leav**es**.

Some nouns have different **plural forms**. For example: woman-women, mouse-mice, baby-babies, and potato-potatoes.

A few nouns have **the same singular and plural forms**. For example: species-species-series-series, and deer-deer-deer.

Count Nouns

Count nouns can be counted as one or more, and take an '**s**' to form the plural. For example: desk**s**, pen**s**, computer**s**, telephone**s**, laptop**s**, and book**s**.

Non-Count Nouns

Non-countable nouns cannot be counted. They usually express a type or a group. For example: wood, bread, ham, bacon, coffee, meat, tennis, volleyball, sunshine, and poetry. Generally, these nouns cannot be pluralized for example: I eat ham, He drinks milk. The sunshine is pretty.

Non-count nouns may be preceded by words such as **some, any, very much, enough** to express quantity. For example: Peter eats some rice. Mary does not speak much French. Chilean wine is very fruity.

Possessive Nouns

Possessive **nouns** show ownership. An apostrophe is used with possessive nouns. For example: Sandy**'s** beautiful house is at the end of the road. Chile**'s** main language is Spanish. Cibolo**'s** movie theater is at the mall.

Collective Nouns

A **collective** noun identifies or denotes more than one person, place, animal, thing, or concept. For example: army, cabinet, cast, company, corporation, congregation, firm, party, senate, troupe, herd, nest, and plague.

Personal Pronouns

Personal **pronouns** refer to a person. For example: **I** go to college. **They** are intelligent. **He** works for the government. The following is a table with the most common **pronouns**:

Singular Subject	Singular Object	Singular Reflexive
I	me	myself
you	you	yourself
he	him	himself
she	her	herself
it	it	itself

Plural Subject	Plural Object	Plural Reflexive
we	us	ourselves
you	you	yourselves
they	them	themselves
they	them	themselves
they	them	themselves

Indefinite Articles—a, an

an—used before **singular count nouns** beginning with a **vowel** (a, e, i, o, u) or vowel sound. For example: **an** elephant, **an** orange, **an** event, **an** article, **an** eagle.

a—used before **singular count nouns** beginning with **consonants** (other than a, e, i, o, u). For example: **a** pen, **a** cell phone, **a** TV, **a** cup of tea, **a** history book.

Definite Article—the

Can be used before singular and plural, count and non-count nouns. For example, **the** girls, **the** elephants, **the** pens.

Adjectives

Adjectives **describe** or **modify** nouns. Adjectives generally appear immediately before the noun. For example: a **pretty** baby, **heavy** boxes.

Commonly, adjectives of **opposite meaning** are formed by adding a **prefix** such as un, in, or dis. For example: clear – unclear, predictable – unpredictable, believable – unbelievable, common – uncommon, aware – unaware.

Comparative and Superlative Adjectives

Comparative adjectives **compare two things**. Superlative adjectives **compare more than two things**.

Commonly, adjectives that contain only one syllable or end in '**y**' use '**er**' to form comparatives and '**est**' to form superlatives. For adjectives ending in y, change the '**y**' to '**i**' before adding the '**er**' or '**est**'. For example: old, old**er**, old**est**; young, young**er**, young**est**; short, short**er**, short**est**; pretty, prett**ier**, prett**iest**. Adjectives with two or more syllables do not change but instead add **more** to form comparatives and **most** to form superlatives. For example: beautiful, **more** beautiful, the **most** beautiful; incredible, **more** incredible, the **most** incredible, etc.

Some adjectives have **different** forms of comparatives and superlatives. For example: far, further, furthest, good, better, best; little, less, least; bad, worse, worst.

Adverbs

Adverbs **modify a verb, an adjective, or another adverb**. For example: It is raining hard. The tea is extremely hot. Smart phones are much faster than regular phones.

Regular Verbs
Regular verbs form their past and past participle by adding **'ed'**.

Base Verb	Past	Past Participle
study	studied	studied
invent	invented	invented
ask	asked	asked

Irregular Verbs
Irregular verbs **do not have definite rules**. Here are some examples:

Base Verb	Past	Past Participle
grow	grew	grown
have	had	had
do	did	done
come	came	come

Gerunds
A gerund (**verb + ing**) acts like a noun in a sentence. For example: Smoking is bad for you; Eating ice creaming is pleasurable. My hobby is collecting stamps from other countries. I like listening to opera. You will be surprised by my writing.

Direct / Indirect Object
In a sentence, **the subject and verb may be followed by an object**. An **object** is a noun or pronoun that gives meaning to the subject and verb of the sentence. Not all sentences contain objects, but some may contain one or more. There are two kinds of objects within a sentence: **direct** and **indirect objects**.

- A **Direct Object** is a **noun** or pronoun that receives the action of a verb.

  Peter buys flowers.
  In the sentence above, the word flowers is a **direct object.**

Direct Object

1) First locate the subject and verb in the sentence. The subject in the above sentence is '**Peter'** and the verb is '**buys'**.
2) Now ask yourself the questions What? or Whom? about the verb '**buys**.'
3) What does the subject, **Peter**, buy? Peter **buys** flowers.

- Sometimes a direct object is followed by an indirect object. An **Indirect Object** is the noun or pronoun for which the action is done.

Peter buys flowers for his **mother**.

In the sentence above, the word mother is an **Indirect Object**.

Indirect Object

1) First locate the subject (Peter) and the verb (buys).
2) Now ask yourself the questions To Whom? To What? For Whom? or For What? about the subject and verb.
3) For whom does the subject, **Peter**, buy flowers? Peter buys flowers for his **mother**.

Present Progressive

The present progressive indicates continuing action, something going on now. This tense is formed with the "to be" verb, in the present tense, plus the present participle of the verb (with an -ing ending): For example: Queen Sophia is **spending** time in Italy. John is **moving** to New Jersey. The dog is **running**. The present progressive also indicates a future action, something that is occurring in the future. For example: My parents are **arriving** tomorrow morning.

Third Person Singular

Verbs take the '**s'** suffix when the subject is third person (**he, she, it**); is singular; and is acting in the Simple Present. For example: Peter (he) drives five miles every day. Mary (she) works for the school district. It rains hard.

Active Voice and Passive Voice

Verbs are either active or passive in voice.

Active Voice: In the active voice the **subject** is the do-er. For example: Josemanuel fixed the computer; **Beth** taught the class; **Gaspar** edited Patricia's book, etc.

Passive Voice: Passive voice is used when the **action** is the focus, not the subject. It is not important (or not known) who does the action. For example: The computer was fixed by Josemanuel. The class was taught by Beth. Patricia's book was edited by Pam. Slavery was abolished in 1862.

Competency 002

This content area to be tested is aligned to a set of competencies that correspond to state curriculum guideline standards, curriculum materials, and research-based theoretical and applied second language acquisition subjects.

002- (A) ACQUISITION: The ESL teacher understands the processes of first-language (L1) and second language (L2) acquisition and the interrelatedness of L1 and L2.

The beginning ESL teacher:

A. Knows theories, concepts and research related to L1 and L2 acquisition.

B. Uses knowledge of theories, concepts and research related to L1 and L2 acquisition to select effective, appropriate methods and strategies for promoting students' English-language development at various stages.

C. Knows cognitive processes (e.g., memorization, categorization, generalization, and metacognition) involved in synthesizing and internalizing language rules for second-language acquisition

D. Analyzes the interrelatedness of first-and second-language acquisition and ways in which L1 may affect development of L2.

E. Knows common difficulties (e.g., idiomatic expressions; L1 interference in syntax, phonology and morphology) experienced by ESL students in learning English and effective strategies for helping students overcome those difficulties.

Source: 154 English as a Second Language Supplemental Preparation Manual
Texas Education Agency – www.texes.ets.org

Key Terms/Topics

First Language (L1) and Second Language (L2) Acquisition	Interrelatedness of L1 and L2
Cognitive Process to Internalize Language	Memorization, categorization, generalization, metacognition, and Bloom's Taxonomy
Interlanguage (L1/L2) Difficulties	Dialects/Accents
Behavioristic Approach	Idioms, L1 interference in phonology, syntax, semantics, morphology
Nativist Approach	First Language Acquisition Theories
Functional/Interactional Approach	

NOTES

First Language Acquisition Theoretical Background

Functions of a Language: A language varies per person, topic, situation, purpose, social class, and ethnicity.

The main purpose of a language is communication, interaction, and opportunity to transfer messages. Language is functional; Children progressively learn how to express ideas (thoughts) or name objects with the purpose of transferring a message. Through interactions with others, children learn how to convey meaning. They use **functions** of a language for the ***purposeful task*** (nature) of communication:

Instrumental: Children use language to satisfy personal needs and to get things done.

Representational: Children use language to make statements, convey knowledge, and explain.

Regulatory: Children use language to control the behavior of others.

Personal: Children use language to tell about themselves

Interactional: Children use language to get along with others.

Heuristic: Children use language to find out about things, to learn.

Imaginative: Children use language to pretend, to make believe.

Informative: Children use language to communicate information to others.

Source: M. Halliday, 1975

Language Development: Language usually begins at birth, when a person begins to acquire language by being orally exposed to it. Children's language development moves from simple to complex.

Stages of Initial Oral Development

Babble: The combination of a consonant sound and a vowel sound that is repeated (3-6 months)." Ga, ga, ga".

Holophrastic Speech: Use of one-word utterance to convey meaning (12-18 months). "Juice" for "I want juice".

Telegraphic Speech: Use of two-word utterance to convey meaning (18-24 months). "Doggie all gone" for "The dog is gone".

Dialects: A dialect is a variety of a language that is characteristic of a group. A dialect is distinguished by its vocabulary (**lexicon**), grammar (**syntax**), pronunciation (**phonology and prosody (*intonation, tone, stress, patterns of an utterance*)**, and registers (**pragmatics**).

Standard dialect: Speech variety understood by all speakers; educated speech; language of the group in power, usually supported by public institutions.

Lect: A social variety of a speech having a functional identity within a community.

Genderlect: a dialect that is associated to gender (males and females).

Sociolect: a dialect that is associated with a social class (or race or ethnicity).

Regiolect: a dialect characteristic of a region.

Idiolect: a variety of a language unique to **an individual** (e.g., different vocabulary, slang words, idiom selections).

Accent: a variety in pronunciation only (**phonology (allophones) and prosody**).

Slang: the use of informal words and expressions that are not considered standard in the speaker's dialect.

Jargon: common vocabulary and expressions used by people who work in a area or who have a common interest (e.g., specific activity, profession, group, or event).

First Language Acquisition Theoretical Background		
SCHOOLS OF PSYCHOLOGY	**SCHOOLS OF LINGUISTICS**	**CHARACTERISTICS**
Behavioristic	**Structural** **Descriptive**	Repetition and reinforcement; learning, conditioning; stimulus-response; empiricism; scientific method; performance; description "what"
Cognitive	**Generative** **Transformational**	Analysis and insight; acquisition, innateness; states of consciousness; rationalism; process; mentalism, intuition; competence; deep structure; explanation "why"

Source: H. Douglas Brown, 1994. Language, Learning, and Teaching.

The Behavioristic Approach

The behavioristic approach focuses on perceptible aspects of language behavior; e.g., the production of correct responses to stimuli. Behaviorists might consider that language is learned by imitation and developed through a system of habits; for every action, there is a reaction, repetition and reinforcement, stimulus and response, observable responses; e.g., if a response is reinforced, it then becomes habitual, or conditioned. ***B.F. Skinner*** constructed a behavioristic model of linguistic in his *Verbal Behavior* in 1957.

The Nativist/Generative Approach

Language is innately determined from within rather than by external factors. Human beings have an **innate cognitive capacity for language**. Human beings have a ***language acquisition device*** (LAD) that enables them to generate language. Language use is a creative and open-ended process, not a closed system of behavioral habits. ***Eric Lennerberg**, 1967; **Noam Chomsky**, 1959, 1965, **McNeill**, 1966* supported the concepts of ***innateness***.

Chomsky's language acquisition research revealed that children **overgeneralize** in the early stages of first language acquisition, meaning that they apply the regular rules of grammar to irregular nouns and verbs. **Overgeneralization** occurs in all languages (linguistic universal/Universal Grammar (UG)) and leads to words which we usually hear in the speech of young children such as *goed, drawed, comed, gived, mouses,* and *fishes*. In Spanish, children say *yo sabo* instead of *yo sé*. Examples of overgeneralizations such us *goed* instead of *went* show that young children do not always imitate their parents. They have the **innate** cognitive capacity to create or generate words.

ESL Connection
Overgeneralization also occurs in early stages of **second language acquisition**. It is usual to hear words or phrases such as She **goed** to the mall, many **mouses**, **sheeps**, in an ESL classroom.

The Functional/Interactional/Cognitive Approaches

These approaches explain child language on the **cognitive prerequisites** of linguistic behavior. They describe language development as the result of the interaction of the child's perceptual and cognitive development with linguistic and nonlinguistic events in the environment. Researchers such as **Lois Bloom**, **Jean Piaget**, **Dan Slobin**, **Lewis Carrol, Lev S. Vygotsky** and others have been strong supporters of the cognitive development (*language, thinking, mental imagery, decision-making, reasoning, and problem solving*) of children.

Jean Piaget: Cognitive Constructivism

Based on Piaget's research, children use language to represent their own reality of the world. Language is a reflection of thought. According to Piaget, cognitive development (development of thought processes) precedes language development.

Piaget's Theory of Cognitive Development from Infancy to Adulthood

Stage	Age or Period	Description
Sensorimotor stage	Infancy	Intelligence is present; motor activity but no symbols; knowledge is developing yet limited; knowledge is based in experiences/ interactions; mobility allows child to learn new things; and some language skills are developed at the end of this stage.
Pre-operational stage	Toddler and Early Childhood	Symbols or language skills are present; memory and imagination are developed; nonreversible and non-logical thinking; and egocentric thinking predominates.
Concrete operational stage	Elementary and Early Adolescence	Logical and systematic form of intelligence, manipulation of symbols related to concrete objects, operational thinking predominates nonreversible and egocentric thinking.
Formal operational stage	Adolescence and Adulthood	Logical use of symbols related to abstract concepts; egocentric thinking comes back early in this stage; and formal thinking is uncommon.

Lev S. Vygotsky: Social Constructivism and Language Development

Vygotsky's research focuses on the relationship between thought and language. Social communication precedes and promotes language development. Child's language development depends on social and cultural interactions with the environment.

Second Language Acquisition Theoretical Background

Individual and Social Factors Affecting Second Language Learning

Individual Variables: Individual characteristics such as *previous knowledge, age, aptitude, learning style, learning strategies,* and *personality* may affect positively or negatively the development of a second language.

The level of proficiency a second language learner attains in the target language is not only a factor of exposure to various **formal** and **informal** contexts, including classroom teaching methodologies. It is also due to individual characteristics and differences; the age at which a person learns a second language, his/her aptitude for learning languages, cognitive style, motivation, attitude, previous knowledge, degree to which the first language has been developed, and personality. (C. Baker, 2007)

Social Variables: The social and cultural background of second language learners plays a very important role in the process of second language learning.

Socio-Psychological Theories

Gardner's Socio-Educational Model (1975)

This model includes the following elements in the acquisition of a second language:

- Social and cultural background
- Intelligence
- Motivation/aptitude
- Formal language learning and experiences
- Bilingual proficiency
- Non-linguistic outcomes, e.g., attitudes, cultural values

Lambert's Model (1975)

This model combines the **individual** and **societal** elements of bilingualism:

- Attitudes (individual).
- Aptitude (individual).
- Motivation, e.g., integrative, instrumental (individual and/or societal).
- Bilingual proficiency (individual).
- Self-concept (individual).
- Additive bilingualism (individual and/or societal).
- Subtractive bilingualism (individual and/or societal).

Definition of Terms:

Instrumental Motivation: Survival within the dominant group, making a living to succeed financially in the new country. This kind of motivation results in ***Subtractive Bilingualism***. Subtractive Bilingualism is learning a second language at the cost of losing the first one. Since first language is one's emotional language, this type of bilingualism may be detrimental to one's whole being.

Integrative Motivation: Integration with the dominant group, meeting new people and new cultures. This kind of motivation results in Additive Bilingualism. ***Additive Bilingualism*** is learning a second language while maintaining the first one.

Stephen Krashen's Monitor Model (1977, 1981, 1982, and 1985)

This model is probably the most widely cited of theories of second language acquisition. This model comprises ***five*** central hypotheses:

- **Acquisition Learning Hypothesis**: There is a distinction between acquiring a language and learning a language. Acquisition is the ***subconscious*** process of internalizing linguistic competence and performance, like the way children acquire their native language (authentic and meaningful interactions). Learning refers to the process by which students become aware of the "***rules***" of the target language, via explicit presentation of rules and grammar through classroom instruction.

- **Natural Order Hypothesis**: ***Acquirers*** not learners internalize grammatical structures in a predictable order. Certain grammatical structures or morphemes are acquired before others in first language acquisition, and a similar natural order is found in second language acquisition. It is predictable that students will acquire the **present tense** before the **past tense**. For example, the third person bound morpheme"-s" (he plays) is easy to teach in ESL classrooms, but research shows that this morpheme is acquired in late stages of second language acquisition.

- **Monitor Hypothesis**: The acquisition of a second language involves conscious knowledge about correctness of a language. *After we produce some language using the acquired system, we sometimes inspect it and use our learned system to correct errors. This can happen internally before we actually speak or write, or as self-correction after we produce the sentence*, Krashen, 1992, p. 3. The learner, consciously, edits or corrects grammatical mistakes, and ungrammatical utterances by applying second language (L2) ***learned rules***.

- **Input Hypothesis**: The acquisition of a second language can only be promoted in one way—**comprehensible input**. Messages must be presented or encoded in a way that the message is easily understood. Pictures, visuals, gestures, and facial expressions work to make language more easily understood. According to *Stephen Krashen*, students are able to do that with the help of their previously acquired linguistic competence, previous knowledge, and extra-linguistic knowledge of the world. Language acquisition is the result of comprehensible input. ***Reception*** (listening/reading) precedes ***production*** (speaking/writing).

- **Affective Filter Hypothesis**: Students must have a risk-free and comfortable environment in which to acquire and learn a second language. The needs and emotional states of students will affect whether input will be readily available and comprehensible to them. It is critical that teachers create an environment free of emotional stress and anxiety.

Related Second Language Stages/Variables

Motivation: The primary reason most of us learn our first language is grounded in the need to belong to the community in which we were born. A large portion of motivation to learn a second language comes from the same sense of need for acceptance and the desire to interface with the new community or culture.

Silent Period or Preproduction: (also referred as Level 1 or beginning stage of speaking) Spoken fluency cannot be taught directly, it emerges naturally. During first stages of second language acquisition/learning, speaking is difficult. Students need lots of confidence in the target/second language to produce verbal speech. There is a silent period that varies according to each individual. Second language learners should not be forced to communicate. They should be allowed to build up **linguistic competence** by active listening via the comprehensive input. The focus in the classroom should be on listening and reading; speaking should be allowed to "emerge"

Anxiety: A lower level of anxiety is desired. To diminish the **affective filter (anxiety, frustration)**, the student's work should center on **meaningful** communication rather than on form. Teachers should avoid direct corrections and embarrassing situations for the student.

Interest and Motivation: Teachers should provide meaningful activities based on the student's motivation and cultural background. Input should be interesting and so contribute to a relaxed classroom atmosphere. Teachers must present as much comprehensible input as possible inside and outside the classroom. Whatever helps comprehension is important. Language Acquisition is an interdependent process. Listening, reading, speaking and writing skills are interrelated.

Internalization of L2 (English) Rules (Questioning using Bloom's Taxonomy)

Cognitive processes used by the second language learner to synthesize and internalize rules in English:

- **Memorization:** Language learners need multiple exposures (7-8) to vocabulary and structural patterns to incorporate these structures in their second language. Meaningful interactions, manipulatives and graphic support are crucial. Questions in the "***knowledge***" category are useful: who, what, when, how, and where.

- **Categorization**: Language learners need to organize new vocabulary (lexicon) and terms or concepts systematically by pattern. Similar vocabulary (***cognates***: words that have common roots) and linguistic structures from their first language may assist them in categorizing new lexicon and academic structures. At their "***comprehension" level***, language learners may use their L1 resources to understand or make sense of new materials. If concepts have been already developed in their L1, students will link new materials to past learning for the organization and selection of facts and ideas.

- **Generalization**: Language learners generalize when they can apply a concept already learned in their primary language. When a student knows that the plurality of a word is created by adding an "s" at the end of the word, then that student is ready to apply that rule to plural words in the second language.

- **Metacognition**: This cognitive process occurs when English learners are thinking about their own thinking and learning activities. Students purposefully develop metacognitive strategies (e.g., pre-planning, on-line planning and evaluation, and post-evaluation of language learning activities).

  Examples of questions at the "**analysis**" level:

  1. What are the parts or features of a cell?
  2. What evidence can you list for the American Civil war?

  Examples of questions at the "**synthesis**" level:

  1. What would you predict/infer from the text?
  2. What ideas can you add to the text?
  3. How would you create/design a new cell?
  4. What might happen if you combined both lines?

  Examples of questions at the "**evaluation**" level:

  1. Do you agree that both angles are similar?
  2. What do you think about the next section?
  3. How would you decide about what criteria would be useful?

Interrelatedness of First-and Second-Language Acquisition (L1 – L2)

Cognitive Theories of Bilingualism

To fully understand the principles of language transfer it is necessary to be familiar with ***Jim Cummins'*** models of language acquisition; SUP and CUP Models. The theories of Dr. Cummins have been very useful in teaching English language learners.

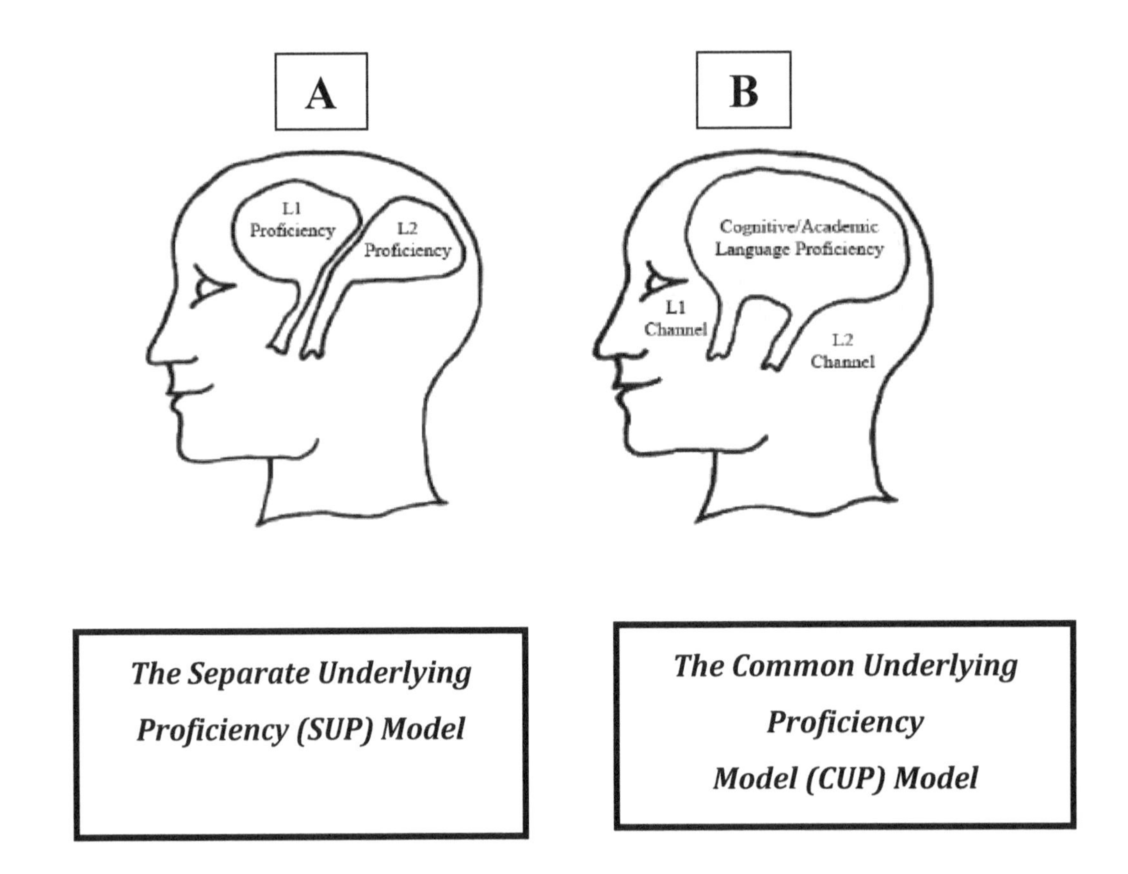

The Separate Underlying Proficiency (SUP) Model

The Common Underlying Proficiency Model (CUP) Model

Model A (left figure) was the model that represented a separation of languages. **Cummins** developed the *Separate Underlying Proficiency (SUP) Model* to illustrate the traditionally accepted theory on language acquisition. The SUP Model holds that proficiency in the first language (L1) is separate from proficiency in the second language (L2). Therefore, skills, knowledge and concepts acquired in L1 **cannot** be transferred to L2.

Current research on cognitive theories of bilingualism changed people's view about language proficiency**. The Common Underlying Proficiency (CUP) Model** represented on **Model B** (right figure) holds that most of the skills and concepts learned in L1 are transferred to L2.

The **CUP Model** is also known as *The Iceberg Analogy* (see below). The two languages are separate above the surface; two languages visibly different in normal conversation. Underneath the surface, the two icebergs are subsumed so that the two languages do not function separately. This model explains

that in surface languages appear to be different. In deep structures, languages are interdependent. This means that ... " *When a person owns two or more languages there is one integrated source of thought" (Baker, 2007).*

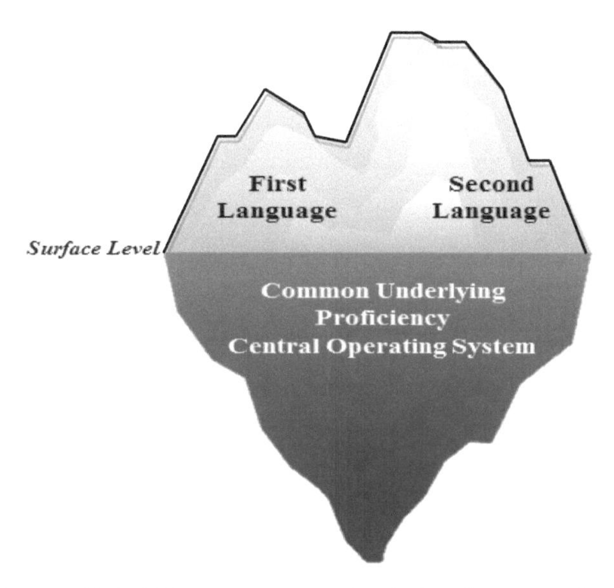

Colin Baker (2007, p. 169) brilliantly summarized *the Common Underlying Proficiency (CUP) Model* of bilingualism in six parts:

1. *Irrespective of the language in which a person is operating, the thoughts that accompany talking, reading, writing, and listening come from the same central engine. When a person owns two or more languages, there is one integrated source of thought.*
2. *Bilingualism and multilingualism are possible because people have the capacity to store two or more languages. People can also function in two or more language with ease.*
3. *Information processing skills and educational attainment may be developed through two languages as well as through one language. Cognitive functioning and school achievement may be fed through one monolingual channel or equally successfully through two well-developed language channels. Both channels feed the same central processor.*
4. *The language the child is using in the classroom needs to be sufficiently well developed to be able to process the cognitive challenges of the classroom.*
5. *Speaking, listening, reading, or writing in the first or the second language help the whole cognitive system to develop.*
6. *When one or both languages are not functioning fully (e.g., because of pressure to replace the home language with the majority language), cognitive functioning and academic performance may be negatively affected.*

Research about the relationship of a native language (L1) and English (L2) acquisition in the United States shows the positive influence of the first language (L1) on ***English*** language learning. Most of intellectual and academic skills that English language learners need to succeed in school (literacy development, concept formation, subject knowledge, and learning strategies in L1) will transfer to L2.

The Threshold Theory, *Cummins, 1979*

This theory addresses the relationship between ***cognition*** and degree of ***bilingualism***. The author best explains the research on cognition and bilingualism as having two thresholds: the first threshold is a level for a child to reach to avoid negative effects of bilingualism; the second one is a level required to experience the positive effects of bilingualism. The Threshold theory may be a house with three floor levels (see figure below), indicating that a language learner is always moving up.

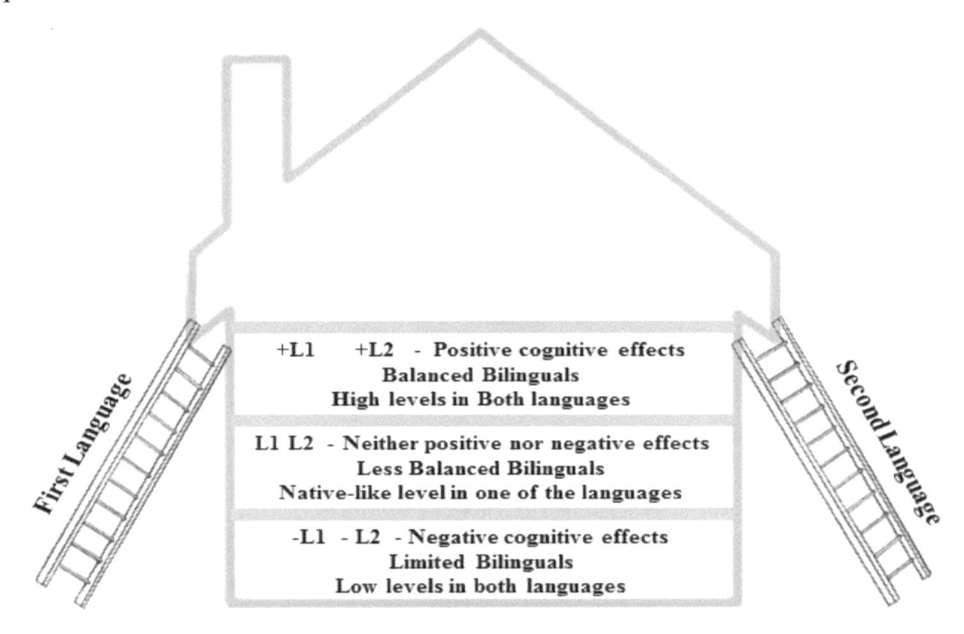

On the **bottom floor** of the house we find language learners whose current competence and performance in both their languages (L1 and L2) is insufficiently developed when compared with other learner groups of the same group. Therefore, when a person has insufficient levels of competence in both languages, there may be negative cognitive effects. In **the middle floor,** will be language learners with age-appropriate competence in one of their languages but not in both. The positive aspect of being native-like competent in just one language, may become **neutral (neither positive nor negative)** unless instruction is designed to help students transfer linguistic and academic skills from L1 to L2. On the **third floor**, will be those with age-appropriate competence in two or more languages. When students have balanced or high levels of bilingualism in both languages, there is a positive cognitive effect. In other words, balanced bilinguals have enough linguistic and academic resources in both languages; therefore, they can cope with grade-level material in either of their languages.

The Developmental Interdependence Hypothesis, *Cummins 1978*

This hypothesis suggests that a child's second language competence depends in part on the level of competence already achieved in the first language. The more developed the first language, the easier it will be to develop the second language. For example, students who read in their first language (L1) have a base of knowledge that can be used to transfer meaning into the second language (L2). Skills developed in first language literacy are transferred to the second language. These skills form the base to succeed academically in the target language. When a child's first language is insufficiently developed when compared to students of the same age group, it is more difficult to achieve full bilingualism.

The Distinction between Basic Interpersonal Communication Skills (BICS), and Cognitive/Academic Language Proficiency (CALP), *Cummins 1984*

The distinction between surface fluency language and academic skills required to benefit from the education process proposed by *Jim Cummins* has also been portrayed as an iceberg (see figure).

On the ***surface*** of the iceberg are language skills such as ***comprehension***, ***speaking***, **pronunciation**, ***vocabulary***, ***grammar***. ***Below*** the surface are the skills of ***analysis*** and ***synthesis***; language skills of ***meaning*** and ***creative composition***.

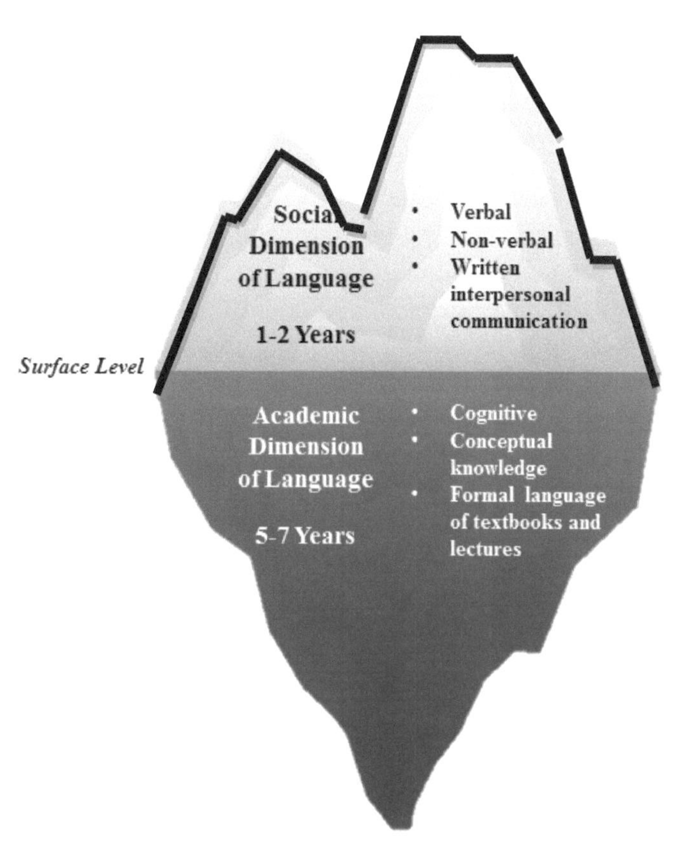

Basic Interpersonal Communication Skills (BICS): Students develop basic interpersonal communication skills approximately within **2 years** after initial exposure to the new language.

Cognitive and Academic Language Proficiency (CALP): Students develop Cognitive Academic Language Proficiency within **5-7 years**, without ESL methods. This process can be accelerated with the use of appropriate ESL teaching methodology such as ***Sheltered Instruction***. *The term sheltered instruction is discussed in competencies 3 and 8.*

Dr. Cummins indicates that everyday speech as *Basic Interpersonal Communication Skills* or "BICS." BICS are used most often when topics discussed are **cognitively undemanding** and **context embedded**. Gestures, facial expressions, pictures, and a sense of "being there" all contribute to the meaning of the messages being shared between individuals.

He also refers to the use of academic, highly specialized language as Cognitive Academic Language Proficiency or "CALP." CALP is used most often when topics discussed are **cognitively demanding** and **context reduced**. Few cues are provided to help one determine the meaning of implied messages. This includes the language of the disciplines and the specialized languages of all academic subjects: math, science, and social studies.

Saville-Troike (1997) suggests that it is important to recognize that there is a qualitative difference between the communication skills that English language learners find effective for meeting their social needs and goals and those that are necessary for achieving academic success in the classroom.

Prism Model of Language Acquisition for School, Thomas and Collier (1997)

This model supports Cummins's developmental interdependence hypothesis that suggests that the development of the first language promotes the development of academic achievement in a second language. Supporters of this model argue that educational institutions should provide English language learners with cognitively complex academic instruction in the first language for as long as possible, while providing cognitively complex academic instruction through the second language for part of the school day.

Language Acquisition for School

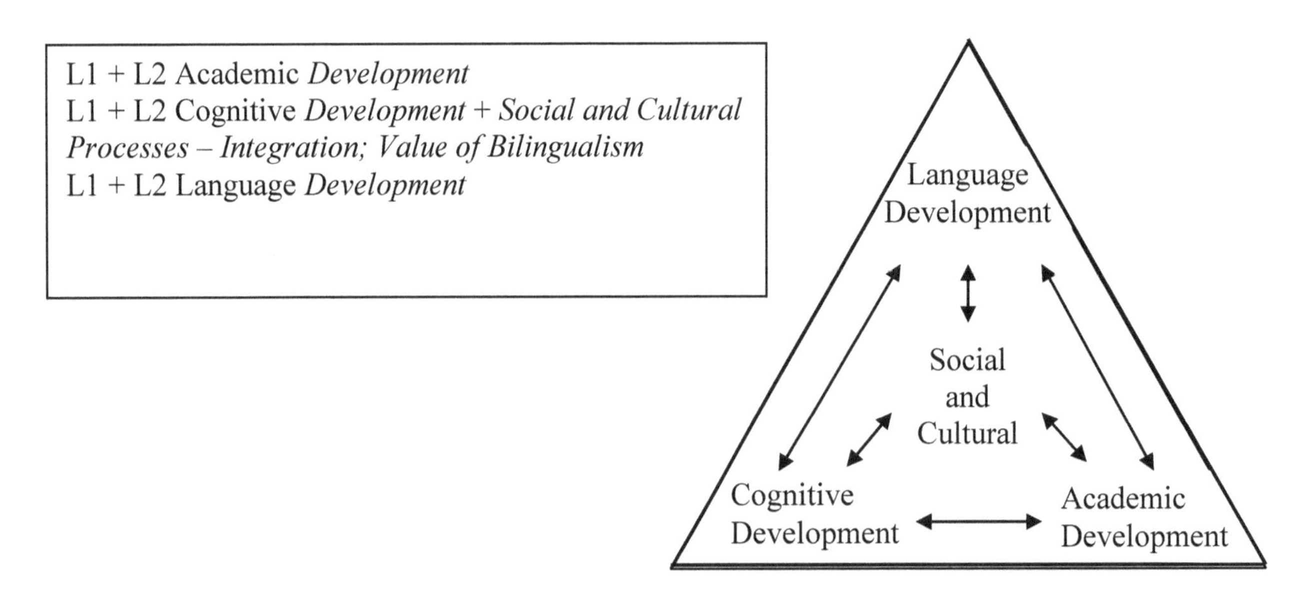

ESL Connection
Knowledge of academic material and academic skills are strong indicators of academic success in any language.

DOMAIN II

ESL INSTRUCTION AND ASSESSMENT

Competency 003

This content area to be tested is aligned to a set of competencies that correspond to state curriculum guideline standards, curriculum materials, and research-based theoretical and applied second language acquisition subjects.

003 - (M) METHODS: The ESL teacher understands ESL teaching methods and uses this knowledge to plan and implement effective, developmentally appropriate instruction.

The beginning ESL teacher:

A. Knows applicable Texas Essential Knowledge and Skills (TEKS) and the English Language Proficiency Standards (ELPS) and knows how to design and implement appropriate instruction to address the domains of listening, speaking, reading, and writing.

B. Knows effective instructional methods and techniques for the ESL classroom, and selects and uses instructional methods, resources and materials appropriate for addressing specified instructional goals and promoting learning in students with diverse characteristics and needs.

C. Applies knowledge of effective practices, resources and materials for providing content-based ESL instruction, engaging students in critical thinking and fostering students' communicative competence.

D. Knows how to integrate technological tools and resources into the instructional processes to facilitate and enhance student learning.

E. Applies effective classroom management and teaching strategies for a variety of ESL environments and situations.

Source: 154 English as a Second Language Supplemental Preparation Manual
Texas Education Agency – www.texes.ets.org

Key Terms/Topics

Effective Practices, Resources, and Materials
Teaching Strategies
Instructional Methods/Approaches
Technology Integration
English Language Proficiency Standards (ELPS) – TEKS

NOTES

Effective Practices, Resources, and Materials

Bilingual and ESL teachers understand that methodologies, effective practices/approaches, resources, and materials should address students' ***affective, linguistic***, and ***cognitive*** needs.

Clarification of Terms:

Affective Needs: ESL students need to learn in a classroom environment which provides self-assurance, confidence, and a positive identity with their cultural heritage.

Linguistic Needs: ESL students shall be provided intensive instruction to develop social and academic proficiency in the comprehension, speaking, reading, and writing of the English language.

Cognitive Needs: ESL students shall be provided high-quality instruction in English in all subjects through effective second language acquisition methods, and the incorporation of the *English Language Proficiency Standards* (ELPS). Students should be able to develop ***academic achievement*** as well as ***English proficiency***.

From Theory

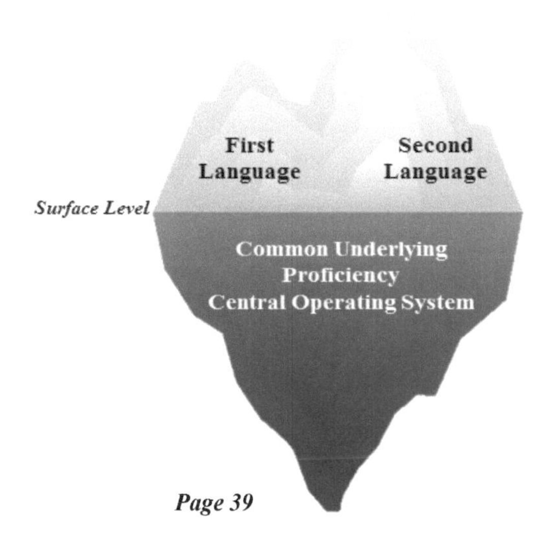

To Practice

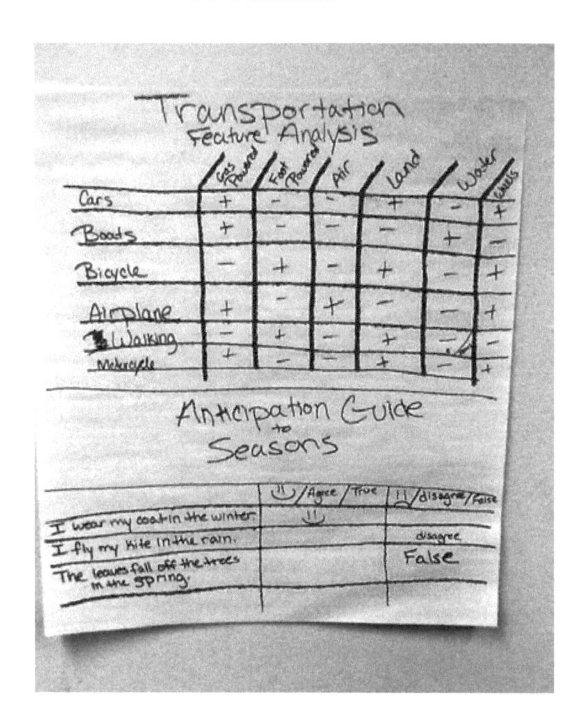

Affective Support – Linguistic Support – Cognitive Support

Suggestions to provide Affective support:

- Pronounce the student's name correctly.
- Establish routines. Give students many opportunities for interaction.
- Celebrate your students' cultures. Involve families/community.
- Use multisensory teaching methods for comprehensible input.
- Be patient/kind and understanding.
- Create a positive nurturing environment inside and outside the classroom.
- Be positive/praise.
- Create opportunities for positive interaction.

Suggestions to provide Linguistic support:

- Enunciate/articulate clearly. Pronounce words constantly. Model sentences.
- Avoid slang and idioms when they interfere with communication. Paraphrase, explain.
- Provide enough wait time. Give opportunities for discussion with peers.
- Post **key vocabulary**. Write legibly. Concepts/terms should be **pronounced** and **written** for students **to see**.
- Use gestures/body language/pantomime to enhance understanding.
- Paraphrase, rephrase often. **Repetition** is **not redundancy**; it facilitates **internalization**.
- Provide L1 and L2 resources (e.g., dictionaries, glossaries, illustrated content dictionary, technology, and native language textbook, if necessary).
- Incorporate manipulatives and real-life objects (**realia**) into lessons.
- Highlight **relevant** information. Chunk information for better comprehension.
- Label many parts in the classroom with English vocabulary. Word walls of **key words**.

Suggestions to provide Cognitive support:

- Use games to reinforce concepts. Role-playing for oral communication and concept internalization.
- Scaffold and build from prior knowledge. Check often for understanding.
- Provide multiple and meaningful opportunities to engage in a concept.
- Encourage the use of tables, charts, outlines, T-charts, etc.
- Provide use of manipulatives or concrete items.
- Enhance group interaction, teacher interaction, and student to student interaction.
- Use pre-reading (predictions), during reading (thinking aloud), and after reading (confirmation of predictions) techniques to set purpose for reading.
- Allow the use of L1 for conceptual understanding and support; peers, dictionaries, glossaries, computer programs, textbooks, etc.
- Use graphic organizers to introduce and reinforce academic concepts.
- Encourage student use of language in social and academic settings.

Language Instructional Methods/Approaches

THE GRAMMAR TRANSLATION METHOD: It is considered a "**traditional**" method that does not have enough literature or research to justify its practical application in classrooms. It was popular in the 19th century and the original pedagogical emphasis was on **reading** and **writing** skills, with little concern for oral language and pronunciation. Classes were taught in the **mother tongue (L1)**; with little active use of the second language. Vocabulary words were taught in the form of isolated lists. Grammar provided the rules for putting words together where form and inflection of words were emphasized.

THE GOUIN AND THE SERIES METHOD: This is a language-teaching methodology proposed by the French, ***François Gouin*** by the end of the 19th century. The main goal of this method was to teach learners the language directly (**without translation**) and conceptually (without grammatical rules and syntactical explanations), with a series of connected sentences that are easy to understand.

THE DIRECT METHOD: Popularized by **Charles Berlitz**, and was referred as the *Berlitz Method.* The emphasis was on natural language acquisition. It involved demonstration by teacher on role-playing through active use of pictures, films, tapes, and other visuals. **Stress on total immersion in L2 with no use of L1**. By the end of the first quarter of the 20th century, the use of the ***Direct Method*** had lost popularity in the United States and around the world.

THE AUDIOLINGUAL METHOD (ALM): This method became popular in Europe in the first half of the 20th century. When World War II ended, the United States realized that American soldiers had certain linguistic disadvantages; most were not orally proficient in a second language. As a national language-teaching revolution, the US military funded and provided intensive language programs to soldiers [known as the Army Specialized Training Program (ASTP)]. These programs focused on **aural/oral** (*listening/speaking*) skills which were the main characteristics of the **ALM**. This method was based on theories from **structural linguistics** and **behavioral psychology** (Skinner); taught through **mimicry**, **memorization**, and **manipulation drills**. Emphasis was placed on isolated grammar structures sequenced carefully to prevent student errors, and included the use of tapes, language labs, and visual aids.

THE COGNITIVE CODE LEARNING (*COGNITIVE APPROACH*): This approach emphasized a **conscious awareness of rules** and their applications in second language learning. Language learning was understood as a **creative cognitive process** rather than a patterned, predictable one that can be manipulated with conditioning. In the 1960s, the age of the **Audiolingual Method** lost popularity among teachers who were influenced by the **Chomskyan** revolution that brought a new perspective to language acquisition. This approach gave emphasis on all four language-learning skills (listening, speaking, reading, and writing), and vocabulary building. The use of the **mother tongue** (L1) was permitted.

COMMUNITY LANGUAGE LEARNING (CLL): This approach became popular in the 1970's and addresses the view of "**counseling-learning**". Students and teachers join to facilitate learning in a context of valuing everyone in the group. The teacher acts as a **counselor** and centers his or her attention on the students and their needs. Students were perceived as a "**group**" rather than a class. CLL teachers were perceived as "counselors", who were always taking care of students' needs.

SUGGESTOPEDIA: This method was developed by the Bulgarian psychologist **Georgi Lozanov** in 1979. According to Lozanov, human beings are capable of processing great quantities of material, if they are provided with the appropriate **conditions for learning** such as **relaxation.** Suggestopedia teachers create states of minds for maximum retention of material in the second language: a) emphasis on childlike experimentation with L2; b) strong use of L2 for explanations and discussions; c) encourages **lack of inhibition and natural language acquisition**, and d) authority figure decides instructional program.

THE SILENT WAY: This method, based on a more 'humanistic" way of teaching was developed by **Caleb Gattegno** in the 1970's. This method encourages natural language acquisition through experimentation of sequenced exercises for **meaningful communication**. The Silent Way addresses **discovery-learning procedures**. **Gattegno** believed that learners should develop **independence** and **responsibility**, and cooperate with others in the process of solving language problems. The teachers' role was to facilitate students' learning and discovering. For example, teachers provided a vocabulary word, a sentence, or an expression, and then students were responsible to refine pronunciation and comprehension among themselves.

THE TOTAL PHYSICAL RESPONSE (TPR): This teaching methodology developed by **James Asher** in 1977 focused on the idea that children do a lot of **listening before producing verbal speech** or speaking. This method is useful for both adults and children in **early stages of L2** learning. Teacher gives commands (imperative moods) and models the physical movement to carry out the command. TPR focuses on **listening and comprehension** by responding to commands with appropriate physical movement in early stages.

THE NATURAL APPROACH This method was developed **by Stephen Krashen** and **Tracy D. Terrel** in 1983. The philosophy behind this methodology focuses on teaching communicative skills, both oral and written and is based on Stephen Krashen's theory of language acquisition which assumes that speech emerges in four stages: (1) **preproduction** (development of listening comprehension skills), (2) **early production** (development of two-words or short phrases), (3) **speech emergence** (development of long phrases and sentences), and (4) **intermediate fluency** (development of meaningful conversation). Techniques focus on providing a context in the classroom for **natural language acquisition** to occur to acquire the maximum comprehensible input. The emphasis is on speech through the creation of low-anxiety situations (affective filter). The 'silent period" (delay of oral production) has been a topic of criticism of this approach.

Language Instructional Methods/Approaches (Cont.)

NOTIONAL-FUNCTIONAL SYLLABUS (NFS) Developed by **J.A. Van Ek & L.G. Alexander** in 1975, this approach (syllabus) is based on the theory that language is acquired through exposure to **meaningful and comprehensible messages**, rather than through the formal study of grammar and vocabulary. The NFS accelerated the development of **communicative** textbooks and materials in language courses. This method focuses on the student's ability to **effectively communicate in diverse real-life context**. For example, the notion or concept of shopping requires different language functions such as size, weight, color, price, etc.

Source: Adapted from Kottler E., Kotter J. & Street C. 2008.

English as a Second Language (ESL) Programs

Content-Based ESL: A model for ESL teaching that integrates language and content instruction in the ESL classroom. This model, also a **required** program in the state of Texas, serves **only students identified as English Language Learners** (ELLs) by providing a **full-time ESL certified teacher**. The **ESL instruction** is integrated with **subject matter instruction**. Therefore, English Language Learners' instruction not only focuses on learning English as a second language, but also uses that language (L2) as a vehicle to learn science, math, social studies, or any other academic disciplines.

Content-based ESL teachers incorporate the English Language Proficiency Standards (ELPS), while they make content accessible to ELLs. Students either share the same native language or are from different language backgrounds. Content is adapted to the students' proficiency level, and supplemented by technology, visual support, body language, and L1 support through dictionaries, glossaries, and peer interaction.

Pull-Out ESL: This model, a **required** program in Texas, serves **only students identified as English Language Learners** (ELLs) by assigning an **ESL certified part-time teacher** who provides only **English language arts instruction in a pull-out delivery instructional setting**, while English Language Learner(s) remain in the mainstream classroom for content area instruction. Students either share the same native language or are from different language backgrounds. English (students' L2) is adapted to the students' proficiency level, and supplemented by technology, visual support, body language, L1 support through dictionaries, glossaries, and peer interaction.

ESL Instructional Methodologies

Sheltered Instruction: An ESL approach that focuses on making grade-level academic content more accessible for English language learners while at the same time promoting their English language proficiency. Teachers adjust the language and content demands of the lesson in many ways, such as **modifying speech, and tone, using context clues**, **modeling extensively**, **relating instruction to student experience and background knowledge**. They also **use social, cognitive, and metacognitive learning strategies** such as graphic organizers, manipulatives, roleplaying, summarizing, visualizing, and semantic mapping.

Self-Contained ESL Class: Typically, an ESL elementary class with only English Language Learners. The ESL classroom teacher teaches all subject matter to them and non-pullout ESL instruction is used.

Cognitive and Academic Language Learning Approach (CALLA): This approach focuses on **academic skills.** It's supported by cognitive theories (J. Cummins, Piaget). CALLA is useful for ELL students who have developed BICS (social skills in English). It is useful for foreign students who have developed CALP (academic language/cognitive skills) levels in their primary language (L1) and need assistance in transferring concepts and skills to L2.

Sheltered Instruction Observation Protocol (SIOP): This protocol provides concrete examples of the features of sheltered instruction that enhances, expands, and enriches **teachers' instructional practice.** SIOP includes eight components: Preparation, Building Background, Comprehensible Input, Strategies, Interaction, Practice/Application, Lesson Delivery, and Review/Assessment. This protocol focuses on making academic content comprehensible for English language learners.

Newcomer Center: A Newcomer Center serves English language learners (ELLs) who have recently arrived to the United States and are new to the English language. Newcomer centers provide ELLs with personalized instruction to meet their individual language and academic needs. The goal is to quickly prepare students linguistically and academically for participation into mainstreams classrooms. This is mostly used at the junior high school level.

High School Courses in Texas: ESOL I and ESOL II (English for Speakers of Other Languages: beginners or intermediate levels). Students can replace ESOL 1 and ESOL II for regular English I and II.

Technology Integration

Technological tools enhance language and academic instruction for ESL students. Here are some suggestions:

- Use appropriate software to help students at different levels of language proficiency (e.g., beginning, intermediate, advanced, and advanced high) develop English proficiency in social and academic settings.
- Teach students how to use the internet to develop research projects.
- Use internet sites to pair students up with e-pals for developing writing skills.
- Use laptops, tablets, and iPads® to enhance linguistic and academic development.
- Use video clips before presenting a lesson to help students make connections with previous knowledge and past learning.
- Use music in the classroom for different purposes.
- Use videos, multimedia, and other resources to enhance language proficiency and academic development.

Benefits of Using Technology with English Language Learners

- Engage and motivate students.
- Involve students actively, individually or with a partner.
- Build background knowledge.
- Use receptive rather than productive skills.
- Provide immediate feedback.
- Promote higher-level thinking.
- Pair students with experts.
- Provide an authentic audience.
- Offer immediate reference material.
- Stimulate creativity.
- Develop skills and comprehension, allowing for repetition and reinforcement.

Kottler E., Kotter J. & Stree C. (2008, p. 150)

English Language Proficiency Standards (ELPS)

The English Language Proficiency Standards (ELPS), as required by 19 Texas Administrative Code (TAC), Chapter 74, Subchapter A, §74.4, outline English language proficiency level descriptors and student expectations for English language learners (ELLs). School districts are required to implement ELPS as an integral part of each subject in the required curriculum. The ELPS took the place of the ESL Texas Essential Knowledge and Skills (TEKS) in December of 2007.

The ELPS outline the instruction school districts must provide to English language learners in order for them to be able to succeed linguistically and academically in all classrooms in Texas. Implementation of the ELPS is necessary to comply with the No Child Left Behind (NCLB) Title III requirements.

The English Language Proficiency Standards (ELPS) Summary

Introduction

- The ELPS are part of required curriculum for each subject area.
- Content area instruction should integrate social and academic language proficiency.
- English proficiency (listening, speaking, reading, and writing) should progress at least one level each year.
- Level descriptors are not grade specific.

District Responsibilities

- Identify students' proficiency levels using the proficiency level descriptors (PLDs).
- Provide linguistically accommodated content area instruction.
- Provide linguistically accommodated content-based language instruction.
- Provide intensive and ongoing foundational second language acquisition instruction to ELLs in Grade 3 or higher, who are at the beginning or intermediate level in listening, speaking, reading, and writing.

Learning Strategies

- Use prior language and experiences.
- Monitor oral and written language.
- Employ self-corrective techniques.
- Use strategic learning techniques (e.g., memorizing, mapping, comparing, etc.).
- Speak using learning strategies (e.g., requesting assistance, non-verbal cues, synonyms, etc.).
- Use and reuse meaningfully new basic and academic language to internalize language.
- Use accessible language to internalize new language.
- Distinguish between formal and informal English.
- Develop and expand repertoire of learning strategies (e.g., inductive and deductive reasoning, finding language patterns, and analyzing grade-level expressions).

Listening

- Distinguish sounds and intonation.
- Recognize elements of the English phonological system.
- Learn new social and academic language structures.
- Monitor understanding and seek clarification.
- Use visual, contextual, and linguistic support to confirm understanding.
- Listen to and derive meaning from audio resources.
- Understand general meaning, main ideas, and details.
- Understand implicit ideas and information.
- Demonstrate listening comprehension by following directions, retelling, summarizing, responding, etc.

Speaking

- Practice producing new sounds.
- Use high-frequency English words.
- Speak using a variety of grammatical structures.
- Use grade-level content area lexicon.
- Share information in cooperative learning interactions.
- Ask and give information using high-frequency and content area vocabulary.
- Participate in extended discussion, expressing opinions, ideas and feelings.
- Narrate, describe, and explain.
- Adapt spoken language to formal and informal interactions.
- Respond orally to information from varied sources.

Reading

- Learn relationship between sounds (phonemes) and letters (graphemes) in English.
- Recognize directionality of English reading.
- Develop basic sight vocabulary, derive meaning, and comprehend English vocabulary.
- Use pre-reading supports.
- Read linguistically accommodated content area material.
- Use visual and contextual support from peers and teachers.
- Demonstrate comprehension of complex reading by participating in shared reading, retelling, summarizing or responding.
- Read silently with comprehension.
- Employ basic reading skills.
- Employ inferential skills.

Writing

- Learn relationships between sounds and letters of English.
- Write using new basic vocabulary.
- Spell familiar English words.
- Edit writing for standard grammar and usage.
- Use increasingly grade-level grammatical structures in content areas.
- Write using a variety of grade-appropriate sentence structures.
- Narrate, describe, and explain in writing.

Source: Texas Administrative Code §74.4 Chapter 74

For full description visit www.tea.state.tx.us

Competency 004

This content area to be tested is aligned to a set of competencies that correspond to state curriculum guideline standards, curriculum materials, and research-based theoretical and applied second language acquisition subjects.

004 - (C) COMMUNICATION: The ESL teacher understands how to promote student's communicative language development.

The beginning ESL teacher:

A. Knows applicable Texas Essential Knowledge and Skills (TEKS) and the English Language Proficiency Standards (ELPS) and knows how to design and implement appropriate instruction to address the proficiency level descriptors for the beginning, intermediate, advanced, and advanced-high levels in the listening and speaking domains.

B. Understands the role of the linguistic environment and conversational support in second-language development, and uses this knowledge to provide a rich, comprehensible language environment with supported opportunities for communication in English.

C. Applies knowledge of practices, resources, and materials that are effective in promoting students' communicative competence in English.

D. Understands the interrelatedness of listening, speaking, reading and writing and uses this knowledge to select and use effective strategies for developing students' oral language proficiency in English in accordance with the ELPS.

E. Applies knowledge of effective strategies for helping ESL students transfer language skills from L1 to L2.

F. Applies knowledge of individual differences (e.g., developmental characteristics, cultural and language background, academic strengths, learning styles) to select focused, targeted, and systematic second language acquisition instruction to English-language learners in grades 3 or higher who are at the beginning or intermediate level of English language proficiency in listening and/or speaking in accordance with the ELPS.

G. Knows how to provide appropriate feedback in response to students' developing English language skills.

Source: 154 English as a Second Language Supplemental Preparation Manual
Texas Education Agency – www.texes.ets.org

Key Terms/Topics

Interrelatedness of Language Proficiency Levels (listening, speaking, reading, and writing)

Communicative Competence (*listening and speaking*)

Individual and Social Differences (developmental characteristics, cultural and language background, academic strengths, learning styles).

ELPS – English Language Proficiency Standards

Linguistic Environment/Access to Language

Linguistic Interaction

Linguistic Opportunities

Resources and Materials to Accelerate Oral Development

NOTES

Linguistic/Communicative Competence

Speakers can produce and understand an unlimited number of familiar, unfamiliar, and/or novel utterances. They can recognize that certain utterances are not acceptable and simply they do not belong to their language. An English language learner must combine **grammatical competence** with the knowledge of how to use grammatical structures ***appropriately*** and meaningfully in the second language.

Four (4) Linguistic Skills Acquired Interdependently

RECEPTIVE SKILLS	PRODUCTIVE/EXPRESSIVE SKILLS
Listening and Reading	*Speaking and Writing*

The language skills can be divided into two categories: ***receptive skills*** and ***expressive skills.*** The two receptive skills are ***listening and reading***. Students use receptive skills when they are receiving language input. The two expressive (productive) skills are ***speaking and writing***. Students use these skills when they use language to express themselves and their thinking. All four linguistic skills are needed for success in formal and informal settings.

Listening, speaking, reading, and writing develop simultaneously. Students need opportunities to develop all their language abilities through different modalities and technologies.

Oral Communicative Competence – Listening/Speaking:

When students are acquiring oral communicative competence in a second language they will progress through four stages:

Pre-Production (*listening and gestures*)

During the ***Pre-Production stage*** of language development, students remain quiet for some time. They appear to be "absorbing" the new language but they are not producing verbal speech yet to demonstrate understanding in a more concrete way. This is most commonly known as "***The Silent Period***." Students may be hesitant to participate orally and tend to use a lot of non-verbal communication (listening and gestures) such as pointing to objects, pantomime, and nodding the head to indicate "yes" or "no".

Kinesthetic approaches such as the ***Total Physical Response (TPR)*** approach will be **beneficial** for students at this level of oral competency.

Early Production (*short phrases*)

During the ***Early Production stage***, students may begin to use **one word** or **short phrase descriptors** to communicate. Students can show understanding by answering yes/no questions, providing one-word answers. This stage may last up to six months and students will develop a receptive and active vocabulary of about ***1,000 words***. Teachers **should** accept one or two word responses; use pictures and ***realia*** (real objects) to support comprehension, provide listening activities, and begin to foster writing in English through labeling and short sentences.

Speech Emergence (*long phrases and sentences*)

During the ***Speech Emergence stage***, students will use short sentences and make more **attempts to communicate complete thoughts**. Students can show understanding by: using three word phrases, using complete sentences, and engaging in extended discourse. Students have developed a vocabulary of about ***3,000 words*** and can communicate with simple phrases and sentences.

Intermediate/Advanced Fluency (*conversation*)

During the ***Intermediate/Advanced Fluency stage***, students will speak in sentences and phrases with occasional errors in grammar, syntax, or vocabulary. Students can show understanding by: ***giving opinions, analyzing, debating, examining, evaluating, defending, justifying,*** and ***creating***. English language learners at the intermediate fluency stage have a vocabulary of ***6,000 active words***.

Ideas to promote oral development in the classroom and outside the classroom:

- Ample and frequent opportunities for interaction and discussion among students, and between teacher and students.
- Group students in small groups (pairs and triads) per language and content objectives.
- Group students of the same language for conceptual understanding and transfer.
- Group students of different language to promote interpersonal and social skills in English.
- Give sufficient wait time for student responses, especially for students at beginning levels of English proficiency.
- Give students many opportunities to clarify key concepts in L1 as needed with aide, peer, or L1 text.

English language learners' instructional context should emphasize the following:

- Content should be based on learner's communicative needs.
- Students should be provided extensive contextual clues.
- Modify English to students' proficiency level and confirm students' comprehension.
- The focus should be on language content or functions rather than grammatical form.
- Students' creativity and spontaneity should be encouraged.

English Proficiency – Speaking and Listening

ESL teachers should provide many opportunities for social and academic interactions inside and outside the classroom. ESL teachers **should** also be familiar with the **English Proficiency Levels**. Social and academic vocabulary, concepts, terms and expressions, language structures, and language functions should be *linguistically accommodated* based on students' English proficiency levels.

The following chart summarizes the **Proficiency Levels Descriptors** in the domains of **speaking** and **listening**. These proficiency level descriptors comprise all four levels of English proficiency; ***Beginning***, ***Intermediate***, ***Advanced***, and ***Advanced High***.

Source: Adapted from the Texas Administrative Code §74.4 – Texas Education Agency – ELPS Descriptors.

ELL STUDENTS K-12	SPEAKING	LISTENING
Beginning Level	Students speak using single words and short phrases (telegraphic speech) consisting of recently practiced, memorized, or highly familiar material to get immediate needs met. They are hesitant to speak and often give up in their attempts to communicate. Students speak using a very limited bank of high-frequency, high-need, concrete vocabulary, including key words and expressions needed for basic communication in academic and social contexts.	Students struggle to understand simple conversations and simple discussions even when the topics are familiar and the speaker uses linguistic supports (e.g., visuals, slower speech and other verbal cues, gestures). They struggle to identify and distinguish individual words and phrases during social and instructional interactions that have not been intentionally modified for ELLs. They often remain silent and need clarification and contextual clues.
Intermediate Level	Students can express simple, original messages, speak using sentences, and participate in short conversations and classroom interactions. Students may hesitate frequently and for long periods to think about how to communicate desired meaning. They speak simply using basic vocabulary needed in everyday social interactions. They feel comfortable using present tenses.	Students usually understand simple or routine directions, as well as short, simple conversations and short, simple discussions on familiar topics; when topics are unfamiliar, require extensive linguistic supports and adaptations (e.g., visuals, slower speech and other verbal cues).
Advanced Level	Students are able to participate comfortably in most conversations and academic discussions on familiar topics, with some pauses to restate, repeat, or search for words and phrases to clarify meaning.	Students usually understand longer, more elaborated directions, conversations, and discussions on familiar and some unfamiliar topics. They still need processing time and sometimes depend on visuals, verbal cues, and gestures to support understanding.
Advanced-High Level	Students can participate in extended discussions on a variety of social and grade-appropriate academic topics with only occasional disruptions, hesitations, or pauses.	Students understand elaborated directions, academic conversations, and discussions on familiar and unfamiliar topics with only occasional need for processing time.

For full description visit www.tea.state.tx.us

Individual and Social Factors Affecting Second Language Learning

English language learners' individual and social characteristics affect the way they encounter formal (e.g. classroom) and informal (e.g. neighborhood) learning opportunities.

Individual Characteristics (intrapersonal):

- Previous Knowledge (conceptual knowledge, academic background)
- Motivation (intrinsic motivation, desire for learning)
- Degree of First Language Proficiency (knowledge (competence) of grammar conventions, concepts, registers)
- Attitude and age (desire to be part of new culture and language)
- Learning Strategies (conceptualization of learning strategies; social, affective, cognitive, metacognitive strategies transfer to the second language)
- Personality and social skills
- Learning Styles (auditory, kinesthetic, linguistic, etc.).

Social characteristics (interpersonal):

- Family
- Relatives
- Peers/Friends
- Community/Neighborhood
- Teachers
- Culture, Values, Traditions
- School Environment

Instructional Perspectives:

ESL teachers should apply and consider the knowledge they have of their ESL students' **individual, social, and cultural** characteristics when planning their instruction. ESL teachers should approach instruction from the ESL student-centered perspective. Instruction should be ***purposefully***, ***culturally appropriate, meaningful, motivational, comprehensible, targeted, scaffolded, interactive, and real*** with lots of opportunities for ESL students to make connections with previous knowledge and experiences.

Competency 005

This content area to be tested is aligned to a set of competencies that correspond to state curriculum guideline standards, curriculum materials, and research-based theoretical and applied second language acquisition subjects.

005 - (L) LITERACY: The ESL teacher understands how to promote students' literacy development in English.

The beginning ESL teacher:

A. Knows applicable Texas Essential Knowledge and Skills (TEKS) and the English Language Proficiency Standards (ELPS) and knows how to design and implement appropriate instruction to address the proficiency level descriptors for the beginning, intermediate, advanced and advanced-high levels in the reading and writing domains.

B. Understands the interrelatedness of listening, speaking, reading and writing and uses this knowledge to select and use effective strategies for developing students' literacy in English.

C. Understands that English is an alphabetic language and applies effective strategies for developing ESL students' phonological knowledge and skills (e.g., phonemic awareness skills, knowledge of English letter-sound association, knowledge of common English phonograms) and sight-word vocabularies (e.g., phonetically irregular words, high-frequency words).

D. Knows factors that affect ESL students' reading comprehension (e.g., vocabulary text structures, cultural references) and applies effective strategies for facilitating ESL students' reading comprehension in English.

E. Applies knowledge of effective strategies for helping ESL students transfer literacy knowledge skills from L1 to L2.

F. Applies knowledge of individual differences (e.g., developmental characteristics, cultural and language background, academic strengths, learning styles) to select focused, targeted, and systematic second language acquisition instruction to English-language learners in grades 3 or higher who are at the beginning or intermediate level of English language proficiency in reading and/or writing in accordance with the ELPS.

G. Knows personal factors that affect ESL students' English literacy development (e.g., interrupted schooling, literacy status in the primary language, prior literacy experiences) and applies effective strategies for addressing those factors.

Source: 154 English as a Second Language Supplemental Preparation Manual
Texas Education Agency – www.texes.ets.org

Key Terms/Topics

Interrelatedness of language proficiency levels (listening, speaking, reading, and writing) Factors that affect ESL students' reading comprehension (e.g., vocabulary text structures, cultural references). Literacy skills that transfer from L1 to L2. Personal factors that affect ESL students' literacy development (e.g., interrupted schooling, literacy status in L1, prior literacy experiences).

NOTES

Literacy

To enhance literacy in English, ESL teachers should provide opportunities for social and academic instructional interactions inside and outside the classroom. ESL teachers should also be familiar with the **English Proficiency Levels**. Social and academic vocabulary, concepts, terms and expressions, language structures, and language functions should be linguistically accommodated based on students' English proficiency levels.

The ***English Language Proficiency Standards*** (ELPS) should be incorporated into reading and writing. A well-designed reading and/or writing lesson should have a ***content objective*** and a ***language objective***.

Examples of language objectives to enhance literacy in English

- Use of reading strategies to comprehend text by sequencing events on a story strip.
- Apply reading strategies to comprehend text by writing a summary that follows the sequence of events on a completed story strip.
- Identify parts of a narrative by brainstorming a main idea, character(s), and sequence of events on a graphic organizer.
- Write a narrative using a graphic organizer to write a three-paragraph narrative including a beginning, middle, and end.
- Write (or draw) a related meaning for each new vocabulary word selected from text.
- Describe vocabulary connections using the following prompt "I remember the word from what we read about ---------------------------------."
- Use the L1 (Spanish) knowledge of the following cognates: poema and poem and then define the word in English.
- With a partner, speak in the future tense to predict what the next chapter will be about, using the following sentence frame: "I think the next chapter will be about………"

Examples of language objectives to enhance literacy in English

Find key vocabulary	Discuss	Think aloud	Read aloud
Retell	Persuade	Explain	Write ideas
Find main idea	Find details	Underline key words	Compare
Contrast	Define	Summarize orally and in writing	
Read silently	Formulate predictions		

The English Language Proficiency Standards (ELPS) Summary

Listening	***Speaking***
➢ Distinguish sounds and intonation. ➢ Recognize elements of the English phonological system. ➢ Learn new social and academic language structures. ➢ Monitor understanding and seek clarification. ➢ Use visual, contextual, and linguistic support to confirm understanding. ➢ Listen to and derive meaning from audio resources. ➢ Understand general meaning, main ideas, and details. ➢ Understand implicit ideas and information. ➢ Demonstrate listening comprehension by following directions, retelling, summarizing, responding, etc.	➢ Practice producing new sounds. ➢ Use high-frequency English words. ➢ Speak using a variety of grammatical structures. ➢ Use grade-level content area lexicon. ➢ Share information in cooperative learning interactions. ➢ Ask and give information using high-frequency and content area vocabulary. ➢ Participate in extended discussion, expressing opinions, ideas and feelings. ➢ Narrate, describe, and explain. ➢ Adapt spoken language to formal and informal interactions. ➢ Respond orally to information from varied sources.
Reading	***Writing***
➢ Learn relationship between sounds (phonemes) and letters (graphemes) in English. ➢ Recognize directionality of English reading. ➢ Develop basic sight vocabulary, derive meaning, and comprehend English vocabulary. ➢ Use pre-reading supports. ➢ Read linguistically accommodated content area material. ➢ Use visual and contextual support from peers and teachers. ➢ Demonstrate comprehension of complex reading by participating in shared reading, retelling, summarizing or responding. ➢ Read silently with comprehension. ➢ Employ basic reading skills. ➢ Employ inferential skills.	➢ Learn relationships between sounds and letters of English. ➢ Write using new basic vocabulary. ➢ Spell familiar English words. ➢ Edit writing for standard grammar and usage. ➢ Use increasingly grade-level grammatical structures in content areas. ➢ Write using a variety of grade-appropriate sentence structures. ➢ Narrate, describe, and explain in writing. *Source: Texas Administrative Code §74.4 Chapter 74*

English Proficiency – Reading and Writing

The charts that follow summarize the **proficiency levels descriptors** in the **writing** and **reading** domains. These proficiency level descriptors comprise all four levels of English proficiency; ***Beginning, Intermediate, Advanced,*** *and* ***Advanced High***. There are two categories of grade levels; **K-1** and **2-12**.

Source: Adapted from the Texas Administrative Code §74.4 – Texas Education Agency – ELPS Descriptors.

ELL STUDENTS K-1	READING	WRITING
Beginning Level	Students derive little or no meaning from grade-appropriate stories read aloud in English, unless the stories are – read in short "chunks" – controlled to include the little English they know such as language that is high-frequency, concrete, and recently practiced – accompanied by ample visual supports such as illustrations and gestures.	Students are unable to to explain self-generated writing (e.g., stories they have created or other personal expressions), including emergent forms of writing (pictures, letter-like forms, mock words, scribbling, etc.).
Intermediate Level	Students demonstrate limited comprehension (key words and general meaning) of grade-appropriate stories read aloud in English, unless the stories include – predictable story lines – highly familiar topics – primarily high-frequency, concrete vocabulary – short, simple sentences. Visuals and linguistic support are needed.	Students know enough English to explain briefly and simply self-generated writing, including emergent forms of writing, as long as the topic is highly familiar and concrete and requires very high-frequency English.
Advanced Level	Students demonstrate comprehension of most main points and most supporting ideas in grade-appropriate stories read aloud in English, although they may still depend on visual and linguistic supports to gain or confirm meaning.	Students use predominantly grade-appropriate English to explain, in some detail, most self-generated writing, including emergent forms of writing. They still need ESL support.
Advanced-High Level	Students demonstrate, with minimal second language acquisition support and at a level nearly comparable to native English-speaking peers, comprehension of main points and supporting ideas (explicit and implicit) in grade-appropriate stories read aloud in English.	Students use English at a level of complexity and detail nearly comparable to that of native English-speaking peers when explaining self-generated writing, including emergent forms of writing.

For full description visit www.tea.state.tx.us

Source: Adapted from the Texas Administrative Code §74.4 – Texas Education Agency – ELPS Descriptors.

ELL STUDENTS 2-12	READING	WRITING
Beginning Level	Students read and understand the very limited recently practiced, memorized, or highly familiar English they have learned. Vocabulary predominantly includes - environmental print -some very high-frequency words -concrete words that can be represented by pictures. They read slowly, word by word.	Students have little or no ability to use the English language to express ideas in writing and engage meaningfully in grade-appropriate writing assignments in content area instruction. **Typical writing features at this level:** • ability to label, list, and copy • high-frequency words/phrases and short, simple sentences (or even short paragraphs) based primarily on recently practiced, memorized, or highly familiar material; this type of writing may be quite accurate. Use of present tenses.
Intermediate Level	Students read and understand English vocabulary on a somewhat wider range of topics and with increased depth. Vocabulary predominantly includes - everyday oral language -literal meanings of common words routine academic language and terms, and commonly used abstract language such as terms used to describe basic feelings. They often read slowly and in short phrases; may re-read to clarify meaning.	Students have a limited ability to use the English language to express ideas in writing and engage meaningfully in grade-appropriate writing assignments in content area instruction. They are limited in their ability to develop or demonstrate elements of grade-appropriate writing in English; communicate best when topics are highly familiar and concrete, and require simple, high-frequency English. **Typical writing features at this level:** • simple, original messages consisting of short, simple sentences; frequent inaccuracies occur when creating or taking risks beyond familiar English. Use of familiar words.
Advanced Level	Students read and understand, with second language acquisition support, a variety of grade-appropriate concrete and abstract English vocabulary used in social and academic contexts, but have difficulty with less commonly encountered words.	Students can use the English language, with second language acquisition support, to express ideas in writing and engage meaningfully in grade-appropriate writing assignments in content area instruction. **Typical writing features at this level:** • grasp of basic verbs, tenses, grammar features, and sentence patterns; partial grasp of more complex verbs, tenses, grammar features, and sentence patterns.
Advanced-High Level	Students read and understand vocabulary at a level nearly comparable to that of their native English-speaking peers, with some exceptions when low-frequency or specialized vocabulary is used.	Students use the English language, with minimal second language acquisition support, to express ideas in writing and engage meaningfully in grade-appropriate writing assignments in content area instruction.

For full description visit www.tea.state.tx.us

Defining Literacy in Bilingual Environments

"To be literate is to have the disposition to engage appropriately with texts of different types in order to empower action, thinking, and feeling in the context of purposeful social activity..."

Wells & Chang-Wells, 1992, p.147.

"Literacies are social practices; ways of reading and writing, and using written texts that are bound up in social processes which locate individual action within social and cultural processes......Focusing in the plurality of literacies means recognizing the diversity of reading and writing practices and the different genres, styles, and types of texts associated with various activities, domains or social identities."

Martin-Jones, M., & Jones, K.2000, pp, 4-5.

Basic Components of Literacy Acquisition – Early Stages of Reading

Oral Language Development: Speaking and listening to communicate meaning. Before children learn to read, they acquire vocabulary by listening to others and by practicing the pronunciation and usage of the newly acquired words in natural conversation.

Phonological Awareness: The ability to recognize the sounds in spoken language and how they can be segmented (pulled apart), blended (put back together), and manipulated (added, deleted, and substituted). In other words, this is the recognition that oral language (spoken language) can be divided into smaller parts (e.g., sentences into words, words into syllables, and syllables into sounds or phonemes).

Phonological awareness is an important and reliable predictor of later reading ability and has, therefore, been the focus of vast research.

Phonemic Awareness: It is a subset of phonological awareness and refers to the ability to recognize the phonemes (sounds) in spoken language. In English, to separate the word "*dog*" into three separate phonemes /d/, /o/, and /g/ requires the understanding that words are made up of individual sounds or phonemes. In Spanish, syllables are crucial. "ma, me, mi, mo, mu".

Alphabetic Principle: It is the understanding that the sequence of letters (or **graphemes**) in written words represents the sequence of sounds (or phonemes) in spoken words. This is also known as ***graphophonemic awareness***. Considering that in English there are about **44 phonemes** (including vowel sounds and consonant sounds) and 26 only letters (**graphemes**) in the English alphabet, it is not necessary to be a reading teacher to realize that *English language learners* will need effective and sufficient practice at word recognition (e.g., teaching vowel patterns such as: "short" vowel sound in CVC patterns (run, leg, cat) to be able to develop an understanding of letter-sound correspondence.

Print and Book Knowledge: General knowledge of print and book concepts; parts of books, and function and directionality of text.

Fluency: A combination of **rate** and **accuracy** that includes ***prosody***: expression, appropriate phrasing, and attention to punctuation. It is related to listening and reading comprehension, vocabulary development, and motivation to read.

Comprehension: The understanding of what has been read to the student and what has been read by the student.

Written Expression: It is the expression of thoughts, feelings and ideas in written form.

Literacy Research in Second Language Pedagogy

Kenneth Goodman in the 1970's, influenced by Chomsky and his revolutionary perspectives and research about language acquisition began doing research on second language reading pedagogy which was almost nonexistent before then.

Goodman revels four "***cueing systems***" for reading:

Graphophonemic: the shapes of the letters, and the sounds that they evoke. The graphophonemic cues are related to the combination of sounds (***phonemes***) readers hear, and the letters (***graphemes***) they see.

ESL CONNECTION

An ESL learner at early stages of second language acquisition might sound out second language words inaccurately by applying letter-sound association from his/her primary language.

A phonemic instructional activity that focuses on **targeted minimal pairs** may help bilingual students distinguish between different sounds in the new language. Practice and usage of contrastive meaningful sounds (phonemes) in meaningful utterances is essential to improve word recognition, pronunciation, and comprehension.

Semantic: what word the reader would expect to occur based on the meaning of the sentence so far. The key component of the semantic system is *context*. A reader must be able to attach meaning to words and have some prior knowledge to use as a context for comprehending the word. Readers must be able to relate the newly learned word to prior knowledge through *personal associations* with text and the structure of text. Semantic cues become difficult to find for second language learners who are not able to relate meaning to prior knowledge due to lack of experience and/or knowledge.

ESL CONNECTION

Multiple meanings, different connotations (feelings, emotions, real meaning), homophones, homonyms, synonyms, antonyms may impede comprehension for some bilingual learners.

Syntactic: what part of speech or word would make sense based on the grammar of the language. The interrelatedness of words and sentences within connected and meaningful text.

ESL CONNECTION

ESL learners in early stages of second language acquisition might have syntactical interference from their first language. For example, a native speaker of English knows how to combine or arrange the parts of a sentence to form a meaningful utterance, e.g.: I have a red car; an English learner from Hispanic origin might arrange the parts of a sentence form the example given above, by imposing syntactical knowledge from Spanish e.g., I have a **car red.**

Students might misplace the position of grammatical categories of a sentence in the second language by applying syntactical rules and principles from their first language (L1). English learners require many opportunities to practice spoken and written meaningful sentences. Practice and application, through effective learning strategies (highlighting, underlying, summarizing, cutting sentences apart (syntax surgery), etc.) are crucial.

Pragmatic: what is the function of the text. The construction of meaning while reading. What is the purpose of this literary event? Language cannot exist in isolation; it has a function, and a meaning within a context.

ESL CONNECTION

ESL students might have difficulties finding pragmatic cues while reading if they have not been exposed to the vocabulary words in context. Registers, cultural reference, formality/informality are some aspects that may block comprehension.

Whole Language Approach

Goodman in the late 70's introduced the ***Whole Language Approach*** which is a psychological and philosophical approach more than a method, and it is based on the concept that language is **acquired naturally**. The whole language approach integrates listening, speaking, reading, writing, and thinking. stimulating a **natural language learning environment**. This approach includes the distinction between acquisition and learning proposed by S. Krashen. It also includes the two dimensions of language proposed by J. Cummins; Basic Interpersonal Communicative Skills (BICS) and Cognitive and Academic Language Proficiency (CALP).

Whole Language Principles:

Reading lessons should proceed from whole to part. Students need the big picture first.

Lessons begin with what students know; they are learner-centered.

Lessons are meaningful and purposeful.

Learning takes place in social interaction.

Bottom-up and top-down processing

In **bottom-up** (data-driven) processing, readers recognize linguistic signal such as *letters, morphemes, syllables, phrases, discourse patterns* and use their linguistic processing system to select, categorize and construct meaning.

When readers infer meaning, and decide what to retain, they go through a conceptually-driven process or **top-down**. Information processing based on previous knowledge or schemata—allows readers to make inferences: to "perceive" or "know". Schema theory and background knowledge will drive readers' decisions about text, and comprehension.

ESL CONNECTION

An ESL learner must combine grammatical competence with the knowledge of how to use grammatical structures appropriately in the second language.

The Language Experience Approach (LEA)

An approach to literacy development based on the idea that students can write by dictating to the teacher what they already know and feel. Hence, the students' first reading materials come from their own repertoire of language (Richard-Amato, 2005). The experiences of the student are an integral part of initial reading and writing as these experiences become the basis for the content of the materials used in instruction. Teacher provides a stimulus and the students generate an oral composition or story which is then written down. The teacher then guides the students directly through a reading lesson using these student-dictated materials. Students get involved in the experience.

For second language learners who have developed literacy in their first language (L1), reading comprehension becomes possible when they acquire and develop efficient and appropriate reading comprehension techniques.

Strategies for Reading Comprehension

Douglas Brown (2007) cites the following strategies to enhance reading comprehension for English language learners:

- Identify the **purpose of reading**; readers need to be aware of the purpose of reading.
- Use **graphemic rules** and patterns to aid in bottom-up decoding. The use of graphemic rules is essential for English language learners at early stages of language acquisition. One of the difficulties beginners usually have when they are reading or learning to read is making the correspondence between spoken and written language. Teaching vowel patterns such as:
    - "short" vowel sound in CVC patterns (run, leg, cat),
    - "long" vowel sound in CVCe (final silent e) (time, late, pipe), and
    - "long" vowel sound in CVVC patterns (coat, seat, read).
- Use efficient **silent reading techniques** for improving fluency. Intermediate and/or advanced proficient students learn the following when reading:
    - You don't need "to pronounce" each word to yourself,
    - Try to visually perceive more than one word at a time, and
    - Skip a less important word and try to infer its meaning from its context.
- **Skim** the text for main ideas. ***Skimming*** is quickly running one's eyes across a whole text. Skimming give readers the advantage of being able to predict the purpose of the text they want to read.
- **Scan** the text for specific information**.** ***Scanning*** is quickly searching for a particular piece of information in a text.
- Use **semantic mapping** or clustering. Mapping or grouping ideas into meaningful clusters help readers select, explore, and understand a text better.
- **Analyze vocabulary**. This is an excellent strategy for English language learners that have developed morphological concepts, and vocabulary in their L1. By analyzing and exploring vocabulary words they have more avenues to make connections with previous knowledge (words in common such as **<u>cognates</u>**, and familiar morphological and syllabic structures).

- **Distinguish** between **common words** (social settings), **academic words** (academic setting), and **content-based** or highly specialized words (textbooks, requires knowledge of the word and underlying concept).
- **Distinguish between literal and implied meaning.** Implied meaning is derived from processing pragmatic (language in context) information from the text. English language learners (beginning and intermediate proficiency levels) need lots of practice and opportunities to derive implied meaning independently.

Teaching Writing

Writing Development: Writing is the expression of thoughts, feelings, and ideas in written form. It is important to remember that our first language is the language of our emotions. In ESL classrooms, ESL teachers should allow **beginning ELL** students to express their feelings, ideas, emotions, perspectives in their primary language (L1). English language learners at beginning and intermediate levels of English proficiency are constantly working with two language systems (phonological, syntactical, morphological, semantic, and pragmatic). They are trying to use their L1 resources as much as possible. Multiple instructional opportunities to transfer linguistic resources from L1 to L2 and make sense are essential.

Contrastive or intercultural rhetoric. ESL students' first language will affect the way they express in writing. Students should have many opportunities to read, speak, listen, and write in all content areas throughout the day. They should talk and write about science experiments, read their math books, organize their thoughts about multicultural events and authors in social studies, etc. (Beeman & Urow 2013).

How to teach writing skills by traits – 6+1 Traits® Model

The *6+1 Trait*® analytical model for assessing and teaching writing comprises six qualities that define strong writing:

1. Ideas – the heart of the message, the content of the piece.
2. Organization – the internal structure, the thread of the meaning.
3. Voice – the soul of the writing.
4. Word Choice – colorful, rich, precise language.
5. Sentence Fluency – the rhythm and flow of the language.
6. Conventions – the mechanical correctness of the piece.

Source: Northwest Regional Education Laboratory (NWREL) and Harris County Department of Education (HCDE)

Stages of Writing Development

- **Pre-writing**: Brainstorming, discussing, and selecting topics and related concepts and ideas to write about and determining purpose and audience.
- **Drafting**: Putting prewriting ideas into writing.
- **Conferencing**: Working with teacher and peers to discuss and review writing.
- **Revising**: Making content changes agreed upon during the conference.
- **Editing**: Making punctuation, grammar, and spelling corrections.
- **Sharing or publishing**: Preparing and sharing writing on a regular basis.

Ideas for Assessment:

- Copying.
- Keyboarding.
- Spelling tasks.
- Picture-cued writing exercises.
- One-word, two-word, phrases, or sentence dictation tasks.
- Paraphrasing (restating, scaffolding).
- Guided writing (formulating questions and answers).
- Responding to a reading passage, article, and lecture.
- Use of vocabulary in a sentence.

Factors that may affect ESL students' literacy (reading and writing) development

- Interrupted schooling.
- Low levels of literacy in the primary language (L1).
- Poor literacy experience.
- Lack of social and academic vocabulary.
- Sociocultural differences (lack of connection when text or topics are not familiar).
- Linguistic interference at the semantic or pragmatic level (e.g., text that contains figures of speech or words diverging form their actual meaning).
- Lack of reading strategies to comprehend a text.
- Differences in spelling; the biggest difficulty for English language learners since English spelling sometimes doesn't follow the alphabetic principle (sound/letter correspondence) consistently.
- Lack of motivation to read and write.
- Differences between L1 and L2 writing (letters, directionality, morphology).
- Differences patterns of written discourse (contrastive rhetoric). According to the American applied linguist, Robert Kaplan (1966), different languages and their cultures have different patterns of written and oral discourse.

Literacy to Biliteracy

"The bridge is the instructional moment in teaching for biliteracy when teachers bring the two languages together, guiding students to engage in contrastive analysis of the two languages and to transfer the academic content they have learned from one language to the other language. Bridging involves the use of cross-linguistic strategies and leads to the development of metalinguistic awareness"

Beeman & Urow p. 1, 2013

Simultaneous and Sequential Bilingual Children

Simultaneous	Sequential
Exposed to two languages between ages 0-5	Exposed to a second language (L2) after age 5
May not have a clearly dominant language (L1)	Has clear L1
May know some concepts in one language and others in another language	Clearly knows concepts only in L1
Is often labeled as a child with "low" levels of language proficiency in two languages	Is labeled a "Spanish dominant"
Has language skills in two languages that can be used to develop biliteracy	Has language skills in one language that can be used to develop biliteracy

Source: Escamilla K., & Others. p. 5, 2014

Strategies to promote biliteracy:

- Brainstorming, activating background knowledge
- Reviewing existing knowledge and experiences (building background knowledge)
- Focus on meaning and comprehension. Meaning of unfamiliar words
- Making predictions
- Making personal connections and connections to other books or stories
- Questioning and oral discussions to extend understanding
- Expand grammatical structures. Provide opportunities for transformations. Foster metalinguistic awareness
- Expand students' vocabulary and concepts
- Give students opportunities to enjoy reading by developing Readers Theaters
- Develop grouping configurations to optimize reading development; **Interactive Read Alouds** (teacher introduces the text, activate prior knowledge, and establish a purpose for reading), **Shared Reading** (teachers read with students, large group settings), **Collaborative Reading** (students read with students), Teacher-led small groups (emphasis on needed skills), and **Independent Reading** (students read by themselves).

- Use bilingual books (written in both languages)
- Modeled writing. Students need to experience the process of writing
- Shared writing. Teacher and students write.
- Collaborative writing. Students write with peers
- Independent writing
- Bilingual word walls. Distinguishing L1 and L2 similar spelling, e.g., come/come or once/once.
- Poetry

Competency 006

This content area to be tested is aligned to a set of competencies that correspond to state curriculum guideline standards, curriculum materials, and research-based theoretical and applied second language acquisition subjects.

006 - (C) CONTENT: The ESL teacher understands how to promote students' content-area learning, academic-language development, and achievement across the curriculum.

The beginning ESL teacher:

A. Applies knowledge of effective practices, resources and materials for providing content-based ESL instruction that is linguistically accommodated (communicated, sequenced, scaffolded) to the students' level of English-language proficiency; engaging students in critical thinking; and developing students' cognitive academic language proficiency across content areas.

B. Knows instructional delivery practices that are effective in facilitating ESL students' application of various learning strategies (e.g., pre-teaching key vocabulary; helping students apply familiar concepts from their cultural backgrounds and prior experiences to new learning: using metacognition, using hand-on and other experiential learning strategies; using realia, media, and other visual supports {graphic organizers} to introduce and/or reinforce concepts) across content areas.

C. Applies knowledge of individual differences (e.g., developmental characteristics, cultural and language background, academic strengths, learning styles) to select instructional strategies and resources that facilitate ESL students' cognitive academic language development and content-area learning.

D. Knows personal factors that affect ESL students' content-area learning (e.g., prior learning experiences, familiarity with specialized language and vocabulary, familiarity with the structure and uses of textbooks and other print resources) and applies effective strategies for addressing those factors.

Source: 154 English as a Second Language Supplemental Preparation Manual
Texas Education Agency – www.texes.ets.org

Key Terms/Topics

Teaching Social/affective strategies (e.g., group discussion, self-talk); Cognitive strategies (e.g., highlighting, note-taking); and Metacognitive strategies (e.g., predicting, evaluating).

Individual differences (developmental characteristics, cultural and language background, academic strengths, learning styles).

Personal factors that affect students' content-area learning (e.g., interrupted schooling, prior learning experiences, familiarity with specialized language and vocabulary, familiarity with structure of textbooks).

NOTES

Who are our ESL students?

The first step in helping *ESL learners* achieve academic success in content areas is understanding who they are: their levels of ***English proficiency***, education levels, literacy levels in their first language (L1), intrapersonal (individual), and social challenges, and factors that might affect their linguistic and academic achievement.

Curriculum Requirements and Instruction

The Texas Knowledge and Skills (TEKS), and the English language proficiency standards (ELPS) should be part of the required curriculum for each subject matter. Teachers should integrate *social and academic language proficiencies* into their content areas. Therefore, teachers' understanding of ESL student's L1 and L2 linguistic and academic competence is necessary to be able to develop accurate content and language lesson objectives.

Instruction should be:

1- Communicated – Input must be comprehensible

- ✓ Highlight relevant information as much as possible.
- ✓ Use activities that stimulate student's prior knowledge and experiences (e.g., visuals, realia (real objects), maps, charts, manipulatives, technology, art, music, pantomime. graphic organizers, interaction, etc.).
- ✓ Write legibly and label items in the classroom.
- ✓ Give students opportunities to use all their senses to understand new language structures and academic concepts (e.g., viewing, hearing, touching, etc.).
- ✓ Make sure all students understand instructions. Explain clearly.
- ✓ Create attractive bulletin boards.

2- Sequenced – Instruction must be linguistically, academically, and culturally accommodated

- ✓ Link new vocabulary to objects and real experiences.
- ✓ Organize instruction around thematic projects for the integration of the curriculum.
- ✓ Provide hands-on activities and lots of opportunities for interaction.
- ✓ Promote open discussions about concepts (small groups, pairs, triads).
- ✓ Teach academic language, specialized terminology, and/or multiple meanings prior to the lesson.
- ✓ Promote many opportunities of interaction in both languages
- ✓ Bring students' culture into the classroom.

3- Scaffolded – Support students' learning to achieve independency (ZPD)*

** Scaffolding instruction as a teaching strategy originates from Lev Vygotsky's sociocultural theory and his conceptual understanding of the zone of proximal development (ZPD). "The zone of proximal development is the distance between what children can do by themselves and the next learning that they can be helped to achieve with competent assistance" (Raymond, 2000, p.176).*

- ✓ Paraphrase, restate, repeat frequently, using the same sentences until students are able to internalize language structures.
- ✓ Model correct pronunciation, syntax, and communicative utterances.
- ✓ Provide plenty of wait time.
- ✓ Change group configuration (e.g., whole group to small group, pairs).
- ✓ Use flexible grouping.
- ✓ Provide linguistically simplified study guides (e.g., illustrated content dictionaries, bilingual dictionaries, picture dictionaries, and textbooks in native language for students with grade-level academic background in native language).
- ✓ Use comprehension support strategies (e.g., guided reading instruction, group instruction, and self-teaching).
- ✓ Adjust instruction for the different learning styles of your students (*kinesthetic, auditory, visual, etc.*).

Teachers should facilitate students' internalization of new linguistic structures and academic concepts in English through the appropriate and effective teaching of *learning strategies* (consciously developed by student) such as:

- ✓ Use of first language resources (e.g., cognates, similar morphemes, syntax, concepts).
- ✓ Guide students to engage in contrastive reflection/analysis of L1 and L2.
- ✓ Use of strategic learning techniques (e.g., memorizing, mapping, comparing, contrasting).
- ✓ Speak using learning strategies (e.g., requesting information, non-verbal cues, synonyms, etc.).
- ✓ Distinguish registers in English and Spanish (formal and informal).
- ✓ Monitor language with self-corrective techniques.
- ✓ Use new vocabulary in meaningful context and through meaningful interaction.

Learning Strategies

ESL students acquire new knowledge effectively by **making connections** between what they already know (**prior knowledge in L1 and/or L2**) and new content to which they are exposed. Through effective learning strategies, learners can **strategically internalize language and content**. O'Malley & Chamot (1990) divide language learning strategies into three main subcategories:

Metacognitive Strategies	(*Why do I learn*?)
Cognitive Strategies	*(How do I learn?)*
Social/Affective Strategies	*(Learning with others/interaction?)*

ESL students should be guided to apply social/affective, cognitive, and metacognitive learning strategies in both, language, and content tasks. ***Learning strategies*** are mental processes that learners can manipulate and control when they have a learning goal.

Metacognitive Strategies:

- Advance Organization: Previewing the main ideas and concepts of the material to be learned, often by skimming the text for the organizing principle.
- Advance Preparation: Rehearsing the language needed for an oral or written task.
- Organizational Planning: Planning the parts, sequence, and main ideas to be expressed orally or in writing.
- Selective Attention: Attending to, or scanning key words, phrases, linguistic markers, sentences, or types of information.
- Self-Evaluation: Judging how well one has accomplished a learning activity after it has been completed.

Cognitive Strategies:

- Contextualization: Placing a word or phrase in a meaningful sentence or category.
- Elaboration: Relating new information to what is already known.
- Grouping: Classifying words, terminology, or concepts according to their attributes.
- Imagery: Using visual images (either mental or actual) to understand and remember new information.

- Inferencing: Using information in the text to determine meanings of new items, predict outcomes, or complete missing parts.
- Note-Taking: Writing down key words and concepts in abbreviated form while listening or reading.
- Resourcing: Using reference materials such as dictionaries, encyclopedias, or textbooks.
- Summarizing: Making a mental or written summary of information gained from listening or reading.
- Transfer: Using what is already known to facilitate a learning task.

Social Affective Strategies

- Cooperation: Working together with peers to solve a problem, pool information, check a learning task, or get feedback on oral or written performance.
- Questioning for Clarification: Eliciting from a teacher or peer additional explanation, rephrasing, or examples.
- Self-Talk: Reducing anxiety by using mental techniques that make one feel competent to do the learning task, "I can do it!"

Source: Adapted from the CALLA Handbook pp. 60-64

Related Terms

Motivation: Determines the extent of ESL students' active involvement and attitude toward learning. Increases English language learners' desire to learn a new language for meaningful purposes. The learner understands the benefits of learning a second language and drives learner's desire to learn a language to integrate successfully into the target language community.

Transfer: Is the application of prior knowledge and experiences to new learning situations. The English language learner perceives what learning is relevant and transferable to other situations. Student will find learning meaningful, and the motivation to acquire the skill or knowledge will increase.

Prior knowledge connections: Most ***Indo-European*** languages, including **romance** languages such as English, Spanish, Hindi, Portuguese, Italian, Russian, German, French, and Urdu are Latin/based and Greek-based. This means that English and all the languages mentioned above have words that (1) look alike (student/estudiante (Spanish), étudiant (French) and (2) have the same meaning.

Most academic English words used in textbooks have ***Latin*** and/or ***Greek*** origin. English language learners with strong academic backgrounds will use words with a common origin as a strategy to develop and transfer conceptual knowledge and academic vocabulary. These words that look alike or have the same meaning are known as **Cognates.**

Cognates have a common etymological origin. The word *cognate* comes from the Latin *cognatus* that means blood relative. Examples of cognates in Indo-European languages are the following:

English	**Spanish**	**French**	**German**	**Italian**	**Welsh**
night	noche	nuit	nacht	note	nos
star	estrella	étolile	stern	stella	seren

True Cognates: They are words that look alike and have the same meaning.

Examples of True Cognates in English and Spanish.

Identical English	**Identical Spanish**	**Similar English**	**Similar Spanish**	**Academic English**	**Academic Spanish**
similar	similar	bilingual	bilingüe	abolish	abolir
doctor	doctor	music	música	metamorphosis	metamorfosis
color	color	accident	accidente	majority	mayoría
metal	metal	pessimistic	pesimista	speculation	especulación
hospital	hospital	planet	planeta	hypothesis	hipótesis
popular	popular	map	mapa	matriculate	matricular
neutral	neutral	false	falso	evaporate	evaporar

False Cognates: They are words that look alike but **do not** have the same meaning. See examples below between English and Spanish:

English	**Spanish**	**False Relationship**
Carpet	alfombra	(*carpeta* means folder in Spanish)
Embarrassed	avergonzado/a	(*embarazada* means pregnant in Spanish)
Attend	asistir	(*atender* means to assist someone in Spanish)

ESL CONNECTION

ESL learners' **prior knowledge** helps them make connections between the content being taught and the students' real life experiences. ESL students' academic success depends on their **background knowledge** of the academic material, their academic skills, and instruction that is linguistically accommodated.

Graphic Organizers: Learners classify, elaborate, explore, and analyze ideas, concepts, vocabulary words.

Types	Skills
❖ Outlines	Summarizing, making predictions
❖ Timelines	Organizing, sequencing events
❖ Flowcharts	Showing cause and effect
❖ Mapping	Examining movement, resources, and special relationships
❖ Graphs and charts	Organizing and comparing data
❖ Diagrams	Comparing/Contrasting

Examples of Graphic Organizers across the Content Areas

	Language Arts	Mathematics	Science	Social Studies
Venn Diagram Comparing and Contrasting two entities	Two characters Two settings Two genres	Two operations Two geometric figures Two forms of proportions	Two body systems or organs Two animals or plants Two forms of matter	Two conflicts Two forms of government Two forms of transportation
T-Charts Sorting or categorizing objects or concepts	Main ideas/details Facts/opinions Different points of view Pros/cons	Area/perimeter Fractions/decimals Addition/subtraction	Forms of energy Senses Vertebrates/invertebrates	Types of transportation Types of habitats Features of cities, states or regions
Cause and Effect Outlining a relationship	Responses of characters to events or situations	Solving algebraic equations Geometric theorems	Chemical reaction Adaptation Weather events	Political movements Economic trends
Semantic Webs Connecting themes with categories	Roots words and affixes Multiple meanings of words and phrases	Types and features of polygons Types and characteristics of angles	Foods and their nutritional ingredients Types and characteristics of rocks	Types of human and civil rights Impact of economic policies on governments and nations
Cycles Producing a series of connected events or a process	Plot lines in stories or pieces of literature Life cycles in biographies or autobiographies	Steps in problem solving Collecting, analyzing, and reporting data	Scientific inquiry Life cycles of organisms Water cycle	Conflict/resolution Elections in democracy *Source: M. Gottlieb, (2006, p. 135)*

Competency 007

This content area to be tested is aligned to a set of competencies that correspond to state curriculum guideline standards, curriculum materials, and research-based theoretical and applied second language acquisition subjects.

007 - (A) ASSESSMENT: The ESL teacher understands formal and informal assessment procedures and instruments used in ESL programs and uses assessment results to plan and adapt instruction.

The beginning ESL teacher:

A. Knows basic concepts, issues and practices related to text design, development and interpretation and uses this knowledge to select, adapt and develop assessments for different purposes in the ESL program (e.g., diagnosis, program evaluation, proficiency).

B. Applies knowledge of formal and informal assessments used in the ESL classroom and knows their characteristics, uses and limitations.

C. Knows standardized tests commonly used in ESL programs in Texas and knows how to interpret their results.

D. Knows state-mandated Limited English Proficient (LEP) policies, including the role of the Language Proficiency Assessment Committee (LPAC), and procedures for implementing LPAC recommendations for LEP identification, placement, and exit.

E. Understands relationship among state-mandated standards, instruction, and assessment in the ESL classroom.

F. Knows how to use ongoing assessment to plan and adjust instruction that addresses individual student needs and enables ESL students to achieve learning goals.

Source: 154 English as a Second Language Supplemental Preparation Manual
Texas Education Agency – www.texes.ets.org

Key Terms/Topics

Language Proficiency assessments
Formal and Informal assessments
Standardized Achievement tests
LEP policies (LPAC decisions)
Ongoing assessment to plan and adjust instruction

NOTES

Assessment Principles

"As educators, we are constantly challenged to make informed decisions about our students; to do so, we plan, gather, and analyze information from multiple sources over time so that the results are meaningful to teaching and learning. That's the core of the assessment process and the centerpiece in the education of linguistically and culturally diverse students. If reliable, valid, and fair for our students, assessment can be the bridge to educational equity."

Gottlieb, p. 1, 2006

Clarification of Terms:

Validity: The validity of a test (measurement tool) is the degree to which the test measures what it claims to measure. For example, if a science teacher is teaching "forms of energy", the content of the test should match the content domain associated with the construct, which is "forms of energy".

Reliability: The term reliability is the internal cohesiveness of a measure. Reliability does not imply validity. That is, a reliable measure measures something consistently, but you may not be measuring what you want to be measuring. For example, while there are many reliable tests of specific abilities, not all of them would be valid for predicting students' performance in specific academic areas. *An example often used to illustrate the difference between reliability and validity in the experimental sciences involves a common bathroom scale. If someone who is 185 pounds steps on a scale 10 times and gets readings of 13, 257, 95, 150, etc., the scale is not reliable. If the scale consistently reads 150, then it is reliable, but not valid. If it reads 185 each time, then the measurement is both reliable and valid.*

Cultural Bias: Ignoring cultural differences and imposing, interpreting, and judging by standards inherent to the dominant culture.

ESL Connections

ESL teachers **should** know how to select, construct, modify, and use assessments for different purposes. Assessment and instructional design help accelerate content knowledge and language proficiency of bilingual and ESL students. Student needs should drive instructional arrangements and methodology.

Teachers **should** use a variety of assessment tools to determine the needs of students and to identify student strengths. Assessment drives the decisions made in the development of instructional design. ***Authentic*** assessment tools can be utilized to evaluate student performance to drive instruction.

Assessments: Evaluations based on a collection of information about what students know and are able to do. Data is collected, in different contexts and times. Teachers use a variety of methods.

Formative evaluations: Formal and/or informal assessment procedures used by teachers during the learning process. The purpose of a formative assessment is to compile information, specifically qualitative data, about the learning progress of a student to modify instructional strategies and activities to improve his/her academic achievement. A diagnostic assessment is a common kind of a formative assessment, which is used to determine students' current knowledge and skills of a particular subject area. Formative assessments are not typically graded.

Summative evaluations: A summative assessment contrasts with a formative assessment. A summative assessment often occurs at the end of a course, or at the end of specific project. A summative assessment is typically graded. The purpose of a summative assessment is to monitor learning outcomes. Tests, quizzes, essays, worksheets, and individual or group oral presentations are common examples of summative assessments.
Teacher observations, portfolios, test data and other methods may be used to determine student strengths and weaknesses. Assessment should take place before, during and after instruction.

Performance Assessments:

Technology: Use of laptops, IPhones®, tablets, iPads®, video clips, music, etc. to help students improve their English proficiency level and academic achievement. This also includes the use of appropriate websites to help students develop research projects.

Informal Observations: An informal observation is a classroom performance done on a regular basis. When a teacher has a mixed-linguistic ability group (beginners, intermediate, advanced, and advanced high students) in her/his classroom, an informal observation is the most accurate form of informal assessment, because it gives the teacher a more accurate picture of a student linguistic needs.

Portfolios: A portfolio is a compilation of the student's work gathered during a period of time, six weeks, nine weeks, or the whole semester.

Self or Peer Assessments: The use of self and peer assessments in the classroom help students understand that their classroom is a learning community. Students become involved in criteria and goal setting, which help them improve their **metacognitive** skills. They analyze their own work, and the work of others. With peer assessment, students see each other as resources for understanding of a specific assignment. When students have the opportunity to analyze and evaluate their own work and the work of others, achievement usually improves.

Anecdotal logs: This kind of informal observation includes notes about students recorded daily throughout the class or the school day.

Conferencing: Conferencing gives teachers the opportunity to know more about students' language proficiency levels and concept attainment. Through conferencing, teachers assess a student's performance and identify the skills the students need to improve.

Norm-referenced assessments or standardized tests: Scores enable teachers to compare a student's skills and knowledge to those of others in his grade level or age groups in other geographic locations. The test percentile scores (e.g., 98%) are commonly reported on most norm-referenced or standardized assessments.

Criterion-referenced tests: Unlike norm-referenced tests, score show a student's good or poor performance based on a set of skills, a given task and/or a specific domain. Criterion-referenced tests are used to indicate the level of expertise accomplished on teaching objectives or standards. The ESL 154 Supplemental test is an example of a criterion-referenced test.

The assessment/evaluation methods in the chart below may be used to monitor learners' progress, determine their level of English-language proficiency, and adapt instruction to address their strengths and needs.

Purpose	Types of Measures	Examples	Timeline
Monitoring classroom progress of English proficiency and academic achievement	Informal observation Informal reading inventories Student portfolios District-level measures	Checklists Rubrics Student self-assessment Benchmarks Norm-referenced tests	Throughout the year Every 6 or 9 weeks

Language Proficiency Tests, Standardized Achievement Tests, and Criterion-referenced Tests.

Language proficiency tests, standardized achievement tests, and criterion-referenced tests results may serve multiple purposes including: assessing English language learners' language and academic proficiency, placement decisions, reclassification, monitoring progress over time and pinpointing a learner's instructional needs.

Texas English Language Proficiency Assessment System (TELPAS)

The *Texas English Language Proficiency Assessment System* (TELPAS) is a federally required assessment for English language learners (ELLs) designed to measure the annual progress that **all** ELLs (K-12) make in learning social and academic English. TELPAS provides the proficiency level ratings of beginning, intermediate, advanced, and advanced-high for the performance that ELLs show in the language proficiency domains of *listening, speaking, reading, and writing.* All students (including new arrivals) take TELPAS and receive one of the 4 proficiency classifications based on their test performance.

The State of Texas Assessment of Academic Readiness (STAAR)

The *State of Texas Assessment of Academic Readiness* (STAAR) is the standardized student testing program in Texas. The purpose of the STAAR testing program is to test in the core subject areas of reading, writing, mathematics, science, and social studies. The STAAR tests prepare students for high-levels of education. In high school students take end of course (EOC) STAAR exams.

The chart below describes purpose of assessments, types of measures, examples, and timelines.

INITIAL IDENTIFICATION ASSESSMENT AND ANNUAL LANGUAGE PROFICIENCY MONITORING – Bilingual and ESL Students

Purpose for Student Assessment	Types of Assessments	Examples	Timeline	Who
Identification and placement to determine eligibility for program services	**Home Language Survey (HLS)**	-What language does the child (do you) speak at home? -What language does the child (do you) speak most of the time?	Upon initial enrollment	New students and students who were not surveyed in the past.
	Oral Language Proficiency Test (OLPT)	-Stanford English Language Proficiency Test (Stanford ELP) -Woodcock-Muñoz Language Survey -Bilingual Verbal Ability Test (BVAT)	During the first 4 weeks of school	PK-12 students whose home language survey shows a language other than English.
	Standardized Achievement Test (SAT)	-Iowa Test of Basic Skills (ITBS) -Stanford Achievement Test (Stanford 10) Aprenda		Students in grades 2-12 **ONLY,** after they have taken the OLPT.
Monitoring progress of English proficiency levels	**Texas English Language Proficiency Assessment System (TELPAS)**	TELPAS measures listening, speaking, reading, and writing proficiency skills.	**At the end** of each school year	**ALL** students_who have been classified as ELL (K-12).
Monitoring levels of academic achievement	**State Criterion-Referenced Test (STAAR)** **Standardized achievement Tests in L1 and L2**			All students in bilingual education and ESL programs.

DOMAIN III

FOUNDATIONS OF ESL EDUCATION, CULTURAL AWARENESS AND FAMILY AND COMMUNITY INVOLVEMENT

Competency 008

This content area to be tested is aligned to a set of competencies that correspond to state curriculum guideline standards, curriculum materials, and research-based theoretical and applied second language acquisition subjects.

008 - (F) FOUNDATION: The ESL teacher understands the foundations of ESL education and types of ESL programs.

The beginning ESL teacher:

A. Knows the historical, theoretical and policy foundations of ESL education and uses this knowledge to plan, implement and advocate for effective ESL programs.

B. Knows types of ESL programs (e.g., self-contained, pull-out, newcomer centers, dual language, and immersion), their characteristics, their goals, and research findings on their effectiveness.

C. Applies knowledge of the various types of ESL programs to make appropriate instructional and management decisions.

D. Applies knowledge of research findings related to ESL education, including research on instructional and management practices in ESL programs, to assist in planning and implementing effective ESL programs.

Source: 154 English as a Second Language Supplemental Preparation Manual
Texas Education Agency – www.texes.ets.org

Key Terms/Topics

Historical, theoretical and policy foundations of ESL education

Lau vs. Nichols – Lau Remedies - Bilingual Education Act

ESL programs (e.g., self-contained, pull-out, newcomer centers, dual language, immersion)

Research finding related to ESL education

NOTES

Historical Background

Immigrants brought to the United States a wide variety of languages. During the 18th and 19th centuries languages other than English were tolerated, encouraged, and respected at churches, at public and private schools, and through national and local newspapers. Some of the languages used during this period were English, German, Welsh, French, Dutch, and Swedish.

In the second half of the nineteenth century, English-German bilingual programs. became popular in such places as Ohio, Baltimore, Cincinnati, Cleveland, and Indianapolis. In 1847, Louisiana adopted English-French bilingual programs. Later, New Mexico authorized English-Spanish bilingual education (Crawford 1995).

At the beginning of the twentieth century, many Southeastern Europeans moved to the United States, and public schools were filled with new comers who did not encounter the linguistic tolerance and flexibility of earlier Europeans. This new group of more culturally diverse immigrants' lack of English literacy and English proficiency became an issue of social and political concern.

The **Naturalization Act of 1906** required immigrants to be proficient in English to become naturalized citizens. After the United States entered World War I in April of 1917, anti-German public sentiment ushered the restrictive period in bilingual education.

Several states passed laws prohibiting the use of German in churches, public meetings, classrooms, and even on the street. A fine of $25.00 was imposed in Ohio to anyone who spoke German on the street (Crawford 1995).

By **1919**, the Americanization Department of United States Bureau of Education adopted a resolution recommending to all states that English should be the only language of instruction in public schools. By 1923, approximately **34** states in the U.S. had adopted such resolution.

As Americanization took a coercive turn, proficiency in English was increasingly equated with political loyalty; for the first time, an ideological link was forged between speaking good English and being a "good American." The U.S Bureau of Education became active in the propaganda effort, sponsoring conferences on "Americanization work" and publishing an Americanization Bulleting and other literature, all financed by private benefactors. The goal was explicitly stated: to replace immigrant languages and cultures with those of the United States. As explained by the superintendent of New York City in 1918, Americanization would cultivate "an appreciation of the institution of this country land, and absolute forgetfulness of all obligation or connections with other countries because of descent of birth." Ellwood P. Cubberly, dean of the Stanford University School of Education added: "Our task is to break up immigrant groups or settlements, to assimilate and amalgamate these people as part of our American race, and to implant in their children, as far as can be done, the Anglo-Saxon conception of righteousness, law and order, and our popular government, and to awaken in them reverence for our democratic institution and for those things in our national life which we as a people hold to be of abiding worth."

J. Crawford, p.27. 1995

The timeline below shows historical, theoretical, and policy foundations.

Adapted from: Intercultural Development Research Association (IDRA) and the Texas Education Agency – LPAC Framework

WHEN	WHAT
Colonial Era	The first Bilingual Education schools opened prior to the 1800s, were not public, and were chiefly parochial institutions. German, French and Scandinavian immigrants opened bilingual schools.
Early 1900s	During the 18th and 19th centuries, languages other than English, were tolerated, encouraged, and respected at churches, at both public and private schools, and through national and local newspapers.
1917	The United States entered World War I. Anti German sentiment prompted many schools to end German language instruction.
1923 **Meyer v. State of Nebraska Supreme Court**	Based on a Nebraska act passed in 1919, this court case reaffirmed the Nebraska policy that no person should teach any subject to any person in any language other than English. No foreign language may be taught (with the exception of "dead" languages) before the student has passed the eighth grade. English should be the mother tongue of all children reared in Nebraska so that they may become citizens of "the most useful type" and so that public safety is not imperiled.
1920s-1960s	English immersion or "**sink-or-swim**" policies are dominant method of instruction of language minority students. Few or no remedial services are available, and students are generally retained until enough English is mastered to advance in subject areas.
1963	The first modern **Bilingual Education** program was developed for Spanish-speaking Cubans and Anglos at Coral Way Elementary in Florida. Funded by the Ford foundation.
1964 **Civil Rights Act, Title VI**	Prohibits discrimination on the basis of race, color, or national origin in the operation of all federally assisted programs.

WHEN	WHAT
1968 **The Bilingual Education Act, Title VII**	The Elementary and Secondary Education Act (ESEA) of 1968: establishes federal policy for bilingual education for economically disadvantaged language minority students; allocates funds for innovative programs; recognizes the unique educational disadvantages faced by non-English speaking students.
1971 **United States of America v. State of Texas, et al.** **Federal Court**	This desegregation case centered on the issue of discrimination and whether the San Felipe and Del Rio school districts were providing Mexican American students an equal educational opportunity. On August 6, 1971, Judge William Wayne Justice ordered the consolidation of the two districts. As a result of the lawsuit, the federal court came down with a court order, Civil Action 5281, which eliminates discrimination on grounds of race, color, or national origin in Texas public and charter schools.
1974 **Serna v. Portales** **Federal Court**	The 10th Circuit Court of Appeals found "undisputed evidence that Spanish surnamed students do not reach the achievement levels attained by their Anglo counterparts." The court ordered Portales Municipal Schools to design an educational plan that addressed national origin minority students' needs by implementing a bilingual and bicultural curriculum, reviewing testing procedures to assess achievement in that curriculum, and recruiting and hiring bilingual personnel.
1974 **Lau v. Nichols** **Supreme Court**	Suit by Chinese parents in San Francisco leads to Supreme Court ruling that ***identical education does not constitute equal education under the Civil Rights Act***. School districts must take "affirmative steps" to overcome educational barriers faced by LEP students. Congress passes the Equal Educational Opportunity Act, extending the Lau decision to all schools.
1978	**Amendments to Title VII** emphasize strictly transitional nature of native language instruction, expand eligibility to students who are Limited English Proficient (LEP), and permit enrollment of English-speaking students in bilingual programs.

WHEN	WHAT
1978 **Cintron v. Brentwood** **Federal Court**	The Federal District Court for the Eastern District of New York rejected the Brentwood School District's proposed bilingual program on the grounds that it would violate "Lau Guidelines" by unnecessarily segregating Spanish-speaking students from their English-speaking peers in music and art. The court also objected to the program's failure to provide for exiting students whose English language proficiency was sufficient for them to understand mainstream English instruction.
1978 **Rios v. Reed** **Federal Court**	The Federal District Court for the Eastern District of New York found that the Pastchogue-Medford School District's transitional bilingual program was basically a course in English and that students were denied an equal educational opportunity by not receiving academic instruction in Spanish. The court wrote: "A denial of educational opportunities to a child in the first years of schooling is not justified by demonstrating that the educational program employed will teach the child English sooner than a program comprised of more extensive Spanish instruction."
1981 **Castañeda v. Pickard** **Federal Court**	The Fifth Circuit Court of Appeals formulated a test to determine school district compliance with the Equal Educational Opportunities Act (1974). The three-part test includes: 1- Theory: The school must pursue a program based on research. 2- Practice: The school must actually implement the program with instructional practices, resources and personnel necessary to transfer theory to reality. 3-Results: The school must not persist in a program that fails to produce results.

WHEN	WHAT
1981 **United States v. State of Texas et al., January 12, 1981** **Federal Court**	The U.S. District Court for the eastern district of Texas, Tyler division, instructs TEA to phase in mandatory bilingual education in grades K-12. This decision outlined specific requirements including: three-year monitoring cycles, identification of LEP students, and a language survey for students entering school. It also established the need for exit criteria.
1982 **Plyler v. Doe** **Supreme Court**	The Supreme Court denies the states' right to exclude the children of illegal immigrants from public school.
1983 **Keyes v. School District #1** **Federal Court**	A U.S. District Court found that a Denver public school district had failed to adequately implement a plan for language minority students, which is the second element of the "Castañeda Test."
1987 **Gomez v. Illinois** **Federal Court**	The Seventh Circuit Court of Appeals ruled that State Education Agencies are also required under EEOA to ensure that language minority student's educational needs are met.
1994	Comprehensive educational reforms entail reconfiguration of **Title VII programs**; new provisions reinforce professional development programs, increase attention to language maintenance and foreign language instruction, improve research and evaluation at state and local level, supply additional funds for immigrant education, and allow participation of some private school students.
2001 **The *No Child Left Behind Act* (NCLB) Title III**	Federal funding for English language learners (ELLs) and immigrants. The Bilingual Ed. Act (1968) changed to English Acquisition in 2001.

<u>Noteworthy Legislation in Texas Regarding Bilingual Education</u>

1969	*<u>HB 103</u>* *The 61st legislature passed the state's first bilingual education bill. This Act acknowledged English as the primary language of instruction in school and allowed but did not require school districts to provide bilingual instruction through Grade 6.*
1973	*<u>SB 121</u>* *The 63rd legislature passed the Texas Bilingual Education and Training Act. This Act directed each school district in which **20 or more LEP students** in the same grade shared the same language classification the previous year to institute a program of bilingual instruction beginning with the 1974-75 school year.*
1978	*In November, the State Board of Education adopted the rules governing the implementation of special language programs for LEP students.*
1981	*<u>SB 477</u>* *This Act strengthened the guidelines necessary to implement the state bilingual plan and established the Language Proficiency Assessment Committees (LPAC*
2005	*HB 1* *The 79th legislature 3rd called session amended Chapter 29.0561 to specify monitoring criteria during the two (2) years after students exit the special language program.*
2007	*<u>SB 1871</u>* *The 80th legislature enacted the data collection of special language program models; four (4) for bilingual education and two (2) for ESL.*
2009	*<u>HB 3</u>* *The 81st legislature eliminated versions of grade 6 for reading and math Spanish tests.*

Instructional Program Models

MONOLINGUAL FORMS OF EDUCATION FOR BILINGUALS				
Type of Program	**Typical Type of child**	**Language of the Classroom**	**Societal and Educational Aim**	**Aim in Language Outcome**
MAINSTREAMING SUBMERSION (Structured Immersion)	Language Minority	Majority Language	Assimilation/**Subtractive**	Monolingualism
MAINSTREAMING SUBMERSION with Pull out/Sheltered English/Content-based ESL	Language Minority	Majority Language with 'Pull- out' L2 Lessons	Assimilation/**Subtractive**	Monolingualism
WEAK FORMS OF BILINGUAL EDUCATION FOR BILINGUALS				
Type of Program	**Typical Type of child**	**Language of the Classroom**	**Societal and Educational Aim**	**Aim in Language Outcome**
TRANSITIONAL (TBD)	Language Minority	Moves for minority to majority language	Assimilation/**Subtractive** Early exit and late exit	Subtractive bilingualism Semi additive bilingualism
MAINSTREAM with Foreign Language Teaching	Language Majority	Majority Language with L2/FL Lessons	Limited Enrichment	Limited Bilingualism
STRONG FORMS OF BILINGUAL EDUCATION FOR BILINGUALISM AND BILITERACY				
Type of Program	**Typical Type of child**	**Language of the Classroom**	**Societal and Educational Aim**	**Aim in Language Outcome**
MAINTENANCE/ HERITAGE LANGUAGE	Language Minority	Bilingual with Emphasis on L1	Maintenance, Pluralism, and Enrichment **Additive**.	Bilingualism & Biliteracy
TWO-WAY/DUAL LANGUAGE	Mixed Language Minority & Majority	Minority and Majority	Maintenance, Pluralism, and Enrichment **Additive**.	Bilingualism & Biliteracy

Notes: (1) L2= Second Language; L1= First Language; FL= Foreign Language.
Adapted from: Baker, Colin 2007. Foundations of Bilingual Education and Bilingualism, Fourth Edition (p. 215)

Texas - Clarification of Programs/Content and Design

Bilingual Education

A district with **20 or more English language learners (ELLs)** in any **language classification** in the **same grade level district-wide** shall offer a bilingual education program to ELLs in PK through Grade 5; sixth grade shall be included when clustered with elementary grades.

Adapted from Chapter 89. Adaptations for Special Populations. Subchapter BB.

A bilingual program in **Texas** should address the following needs of English language learners:

Affective Needs	***Linguistic Needs***	***Cognitive Needs***
English language learners shall be provided instruction in their home language to introduce basic concepts of the school environment, and instruction both in their home language and in English, which instills confidence, self-assurance, and a positive identity with their cultural heritages. The program shall address the history and cultural heritage associated with both the students' home language and the United States.	*English language learners shall be provided instruction in the skills of listening, speaking, reading, and writing both in their home language and in English. The instruction in both languages shall be structured to ensure that the students master the required essential knowledge and skills and higher-order thinking skills in all subjects.*	*English language learners shall be provided instruction in language arts, mathematics, science, and social studies both in their home language and in English. The content area instruction in both languages shall be structured to ensure that the students master the required essential knowledge and skills and higher-order thinking skills in all subjects.*

Based on students' academic needs and learning goals, school districts can implement **transitional language programs** and/or **dual language programs**. See descriptions below:

Transitional bilingual/early exit	***Transitional bilingual/late exit***
*This is a bilingual program model that serves a student identified as limited English proficient in both English and Spanish, or another language, and transfers the student to English-only instruction. This model provides **instruction in literacy and academic content areas through the medium of the student's first language, along with instruction in English oral and academic language development.** Non-academic subjects such as art, music, and physical education may also be taught in English. **Exiting of a student to an all-English program of instruction will occur no earlier than the end of Grade 1 or, if the student enrolls in school during or after Grade 1, no earlier than two years or later than five years** after the student enrolls in school.*	*This is a bilingual program model that serves a student identified as limited English proficient in both English and Spanish, or another language, and transfers the student to English-only instruction. Academic growth is accelerated through cognitively challenging academic work in the student's first language along with meaningful academic content taught through the student's second language, English. **The goal is to promote high levels of academic achievement and full academic language proficiency in the student's first language and English.** A student enrolled in a transitional bilingual/late exit program is eligible to **exit the program no earlier than six years or later than seven years** after the student enrolls in school.*

Adapted from Chapter 89. Adaptations for Special Populations. Subchapter BB.
http://www.tea.state.tx.us/index2.aspx?id=4098&menu_id=720

Dual Language Programs

MAIN GOALS	
	Promotion of literacy, **biliteracy**, **bilingualism**, **biculturalism**, and high academic achievement
	Integration of English speakers and English language learners. **Pluralism**.
	Additive Outcomes and additive bilingual environment; high levels of bilingual proficiency. More positive attitudes toward other cultures.

Dual language immersion/two-way	***Dual language immersion/one-way***
*This is a **bi-literacy program** model that integrates **students proficient in English and students identified as limited English proficient**. This model provides instruction in both English and Spanish, or another language, and transfers a student identified as limited English proficient to English-only instruction. Instruction is provided to both native English speakers and native speakers of another language in an instructional setting where language learning is integrated with content instruction. **Academic subjects are taught to all students through both English and the other language**. Program **exit will occur no earlier than six years or later than seven years after the student enrolls in school.** A student who has met exit criteria may continue receiving services, but the school district will not receive the bilingual education allotment for that student.*	*This is a **bi-literacy program** model that serves **only students identified as limited English proficient**. This model provides instruction in both English and Spanish, or another language, and transfers a student to English-only instruction. Instruction is provided to English language learners in an instructional setting where language learning is integrated with content instruction. **Academic subjects are taught to all students through both English and the other language.** Program **exit will occur no earlier than six years or later than seven years after the student enrolls in school**. A student who has met exit criteria may continue receiving services, but the school district will not receive the bilingual education allotment for that student*

Adapted from Chapter 89. Adaptations for Special Populations. Subchapter BB.
http://www.tea.state.tx.us/index2.aspx?id=4098&menu_id=720

English as a Second Language (ESL) Programs

All English language learners for whom a school district is not required to offer a bilingual education program shall be provided an English as a second language regardless of the students' grade levels and home language, and regardless of the number of such students.

Adapted from Chapter 89. Adaptations for Special Populations. Subchapter BB

An ESL program in **Texas** should address the following needs of English language learners.:

Affective Needs	***Linguistic Needs***	***Cognitive Needs***
English language learners shall be provided instruction using second language methods in English to introduce basic concepts of the school environment, which instills confidence, self-assurance, and a positive identity with their cultural heritages. The program shall address the history and cultural heritage associated with both the students' home language and the United States.	*English language learners shall be provided intensive instruction to develop proficiency in listening, speaking, reading, and writing in the English language. The instruction in academic content areas shall be structured to ensure that the students master the required essential knowledge and skills and higher-order thinking skills.*	*English language learners Shall be provided instruction in English in language arts, mathematics, science, and social studies using second language methods. The instruction in academic content areas shall be structured to ensure that the students master the required essential knowledge and skills and higher-order thinking skills.*

Based on the linguistic and academic needs of the students, school districts should implement one of the following program models.

English as a second language/content-based program model	***English as a second language/pull-out program model***
*This is an English program that serves only students identified as English language learners by providing a **full-time teacher certified** under the Texas Education Code (TEC), §29.061(c), to provide supplementary instruction for all **content area instruction**. The program integrates English as a second language instruction with subject matter instruction that focuses not only on learning a second language, but using that language as a medium to learn mathematics, science, social studies, or other academic subjects. Exiting of a student to an all-English program of instruction without English as a second language support will occur no earlier than the end of Grade 1 or, if the student enrolls in school during or after Grade 1, no earlier than two years or later than five years after the student enrolls in school. At the high school level, the English language learner receives sheltered instruction in all content areas.*	*This is an English program that serves only students identified as English language learners by providing a **part-time teacher certified** under the TEC, §29.061(c), to provide **English language arts instruction exclusively**, while the student remains in a mainstream instructional arrangement in the remaining content areas. Instruction may be provided by the English as a second language teacher in a pull-out or inclusionary delivery model. Exiting of a student to an all-English program of instruction without English as a second language support will occur no earlier than the end of Grade 1 or, if the student enrolls in school during or after Grade 1, no earlier than two years or later than five years after the student enrolls in school. At the high school level, the English language learner receives sheltered instruction in all content areas.*

Adapted from Chapter 89. Adaptations for Special Populations. Subchapter BB.
http://www.tea.state.tx.us/index2.aspx?id=4098&menu_id=720

Clarification of Programs and Other Instructional Settings

Content-Based ESL: A model for ESL teaching that integrates language and content instruction in the ESL classroom. This model, also a **required** program in the state of Texas, serves only students identified as English Language Learners (ELLs) by providing a **full-time ESL certified teacher**. The **ESL instruction is integrated with subject matter instruction**. Therefore, English Language Learners' instruction not only focuses on learning English as a second language, but also use that language (L2) as a vehicle to learn science, math, social studies, or any other academic disciplines. Content-based ESL teachers can incorporate the English Language Proficiency Standards (ELPS), while they make content accessible to ELLs. Students either share the same native language or are from different language backgrounds. Content is adapted to the students' proficiency level, and supplemented by technology, visual support, body language, and L1 support through dictionaries, glossaries, and peer interaction.

Pull-Out ESL: This model, a **required** program in Texas, serves only students identified as English Language Learners (ELLs) by assigning an **ESL certified part-time teacher** who provides only **English language arts instruction** in a pull-out delivery instructional setting, while English Language Learner(s) remain in the mainstream classroom for content area instruction. Students either share the same native language or are from different language backgrounds. English (students' L2) is adapted to the students' proficiency level, and supplemented by technology, visual support, body language, L1 support through dictionaries, glossaries, and peer interaction.

Sheltered Instruction: An ESL approach that focuses on **making grade-level academic content more accessible for English language learners** while at the same time promoting their English language proficiency. Teachers adjust the language and content demands of the lesson in many ways, such as **modifying speech and tone, using context clues**, **modeling extensively**, **relating instruction to student experience and background knowledge**. They also use **social, cognitive, and metacognitive learning strategies** such as graphic organizers, manipulatives, roleplaying, summarizing, visualizing, and semantic mapping.

Self-Contained ESL Class: Typically, an ESL elementary class with only English Language Learners. The ESL classroom teacher teaches all subject matter to them and non-pullout ESL instruction is used.

Cognitive and Academic Language Learning Approach (CALLA): This approach focuses on academic skills. It's supported by cognitive theories (J. Cummins, Piaget). CALLA is useful for ELL students who have developed BICS (social skills in English). It is useful for foreign students who have developed CALP (academic language/cognitive skills) levels in their primary language (L1) and need assistance in transferring concepts and skills to L2.

Sheltered Instruction Observation Protocol (SIOP): This protocol provides concrete examples of the features of sheltered instruction that enhances, expands, and enriches teachers' instructional practice. SIOP includes eight components: Preparation, Building Background, Comprehensible Input, Strategies, Interaction, Practice/Application, Lesson Delivery, and Review/Assessment. This protocol focuses on making academic content comprehensible for English language learners.

Newcomer Program: A Newcomer Program serves English language learners (ELLs) who have **recently arrived** to the United States and are new to the English language. Newcomer programs provide ELLs with personalized instruction to meet their individual language and academic needs. The goal is to quickly prepare students linguistically and academically for participation into mainstreams classrooms. This is mostly used at the junior high school level.

High School Courses in Texas: ESOL I and ESOL II (English for Speakers of Other Languages: beginners or intermediate levels). Students can replace ESOL 1 and ESOL II for regular English I and II.

For additional second language methodologies, review Competency 3 of this study guide.

Competency 009

This content area to be tested is aligned to a set of competencies that correspond to state curriculum guideline standards, curriculum materials, and research-based theoretical and applied second language acquisition subjects.

009 - (M) MULTICULTURALISM: The ESL teacher understands factors that affect ESL students' learning and implements strategies for creating an effective multicultural and multilingual learning environment.

The beginning ESL teacher:

A. Understands cultural and linguistic diversity in the ESL classroom and other factors that may affect students' learning of academic content, language, and culture (e.g., age, developmental characteristics, academic strengths and needs, preferred learning styles, personality, sociocultural factors, home environment, attitude, and exceptionalities).

B. Knows how to create an effective multicultural and multilingual learning environment that addresses the affective, linguistic and cognitive needs of ESL students and facilitate students' learning and language acquisition.

C. Knows factors that contribute to cultural bias (e.g., stereotyping, prejudice, ethnocentrism) and knows how to create a culturally responsive learning environment.

D. Demonstrates sensitivity to students' diverse cultural and socioeconomic backgrounds and shows respect for language differences.

E. Applies strategies for creating among students and awareness of and respect for linguistic and cultural diversity.

Source: 154 English as a Second Language Supplemental Preparation Manual
Texas Education Agency – www.texes.ets.org

Key Terms/Topics

Individual differences (e.g., age, developmental characteristics, academic strengths and needs, preferred learning styles, personality, attitude) – Linguistic diversity Social differences (e.g., home environment, community, peers, teachers) Effective multilingual and multicultural learning environment - Awareness and respect for cultural diversity

NOTES

State of Transition

Texas has experienced a population increase of 23 percent, or 4.0 million people in the last decade. This is equivalent to the combined populations of Dallas, Houston, San Antonio, and Corpus Christi. Most of that growth is attributed to natural increase caused by a higher birthrate than mortality rate. As the population of Texas growths, the median age is rising older. In 2000, only 9 percent of the population was age 65 or older. By 2030, 20 percent of the population will be at least 65 years old. In the 1980s, two of every three of new Texans were non-Anglo and 50 percent were Hispanic. By the 1990s, eight of every 10 were non-Anglo and 60 percent were Hispanic.

By 2040, these changes will be evident in Texas:

1. Eight out of 10 students in public elementary and secondary school will be non-Anglo.
2. Seven of every 10 students in public colleges and universities will be non-Anglo. 62 percent of the aggregate household incomes and 68 percent of consumer expenditures will come from non-Anglos. 62 percent of tax revenues will come from households that have a non-Anglo head.

Source: State of transition - Research by Steve Murdock, Former Texas Demographer, Director of US Census.

Individual and Social Variables Affecting Second Language Learning

Individual Variables and Social variables

Individual characteristics such as ***previous knowledge, age, aptitude, learning style, learning strategies and personality*** join with the social context to account for the use the second language learner makes of the formal (e.g. classroom) and informal (e.g. neighborhood) learning opportunities.

Individual Characteristics

- The age at which a person learns a second language,
- His/her aptitude for learning languages,
- Cognitive style,
- Personality,
- Motivation,
- Attitude,
- Previous knowledge, and
- Degree to which the first language has been developed.

Lambert's (1975) Model: This model combines the **individual** and **societal** elements of bilingualism:

- Attitudes (individual),
- Aptitude (individual),
- Motivation, e.g., Integrative, Instrumental (individual and/or societal),
- Bilingual Proficiency (individual),
- Self-Concept (individual),
- Additive Bilingualism (individual and/or societal), and
- Subtractive Bilingualism (individual and/or societal).

Instrumental Motivation: Survival within the dominant group, making a living to succeed financially in the new country. This kind of motivation results in ***Subtractive Bilingualism***. Subtractive bilingualism is learning a second language at the cost of losing the first one. Since first language is one's emotional language, this type of bilingualism may be detrimental to one's whole being.

Integrative Motivation: Integration with the dominant group, meeting new people and new cultures. This kind of motivation results in ***Additive Bilingualism***. Additive bilingualism is learning a second language while maintaining the first one.

Bilingualism, Multiculturalism, Assimilation, Acculturation. Clarification

Bilingualism: Defining bilingualism is problematic since individuals with varying bilingual characteristics may be classified as bilingual. One approach is to recognize various categories of bilingualism such as bilingual ability – individuals who are fluent in two languages but rarely use both, and bilingual usage-individuals who may be less fluent but use both languages regularly. In addition, determination of bilingual proficiency should include consideration of the four language dimensions – listening, speaking reading and writing (Baker, 2007).

The term ***bilingualism*** is typically used to describe **two languages of an individual**. The term ***diglossia*** describes **two languages in society**. Fasol, 2006 explains that the concept of diglossia occurs when a single language or speech community use certain languages and/or dialects. As part of the social organization of dialects of the same language, some dialects are used for formal purposes while others are used for everyday purposes. Sometimes, a dialect is used for writing and another for speech. Fishman, 1972 cites Paraguay as the example of a language community containing both individual bilingualism and diglossia. Almost all inhabitants speak Guarani and Spanish. Both languages coexist in the Paraguayan community and are used in a functionally distinct way.

Clarification of Terms:

Types of Bilingual Students

Balanced Bilinguals	Transitional Bilinguals	Emergent Bilinguals
Competence in both languages is well developed; Fluent in two languages across various contexts; More or less equally proficient in both languages; Able to cope with the conceptual and linguistic tasks of the school curriculum in two languages.	Proficient in one of the two languages (usually the home language), and show developmental progress in the second language; Show fluency or proficiency (e.g., understanding, speaking in some of the second language abilities); May be able to use the two languages for different purposes and events; Do not demonstrate sufficient mastery of the second language to cope and excel with English curriculum standards.	Proficient or fluent in the home language with evolving development in the second language (English in the United States); At the initial process of learning a second language (English in school); Do not have mastery of the second language to meet curriculum standards in English.

Rodríguez, D., Carrasquillo, A., & Soon Lee, K. 2014. The Bilingual Advantage (p. 17).

Simultaneous bilingual: A child who has been exposed to two languages before age 3. When children learn two languages from birth (Baker 2017).

Sequential bilingual: A student who has developed one language and is learning a second language. Children who have learned a second language after age 3, it is considered sequential o consecutive bilingualism (Baker 2017).

Benefits of Bilingualism

Communication Advantages

1- Wider communication (extended family, community, international links, employment)
2- Literacy in two languages.

Cultural Advantages

3- Broader enculturation, a deeper multiculturalism, and two "language worlds" of experience.
4- Greater tolerance and appreciation of diversity.

Cognitive Advantages

5- Thinking benefits (e.g. creativity, sensitivity to communications).

Character Advantages

6- Raised self-esteem.
7- Security in identity.

Curriculum Advantages

8- Increased curriculum achievement.
9- Easier to learn a third language.

Cash Advantages

10- Economic and employment benefits.

Source: Baker, C. 2007. A Parents' and Teachers' Guide to Bilingualism (p. 2).

Related Terms:

Multiculturalism: The appreciation and respect of multiple cultures. Usually, people that have a multicultural view advocate extending equitable status to diverse ethnic and religious groups without promoting any specific cultural community values as central. In this context, a person who has a multicultural view of others has more respect for other peoples and other cultures than a monocultural individual.

Cultural Assimilation: The political response to the demographic fact of multi-ethnicity which encourages absorption of the minority into the dominant culture. This is when the minority language and culture may be left behind to prosper in the majority language community.

Acculturation (enculturation): A general term for the process of becoming adjusted to another culture. It is the ***exchange of cultural features*** that results when groups or individuals reciprocally adopt or appreciate the attitudes, the values, traditions, beliefs, and language patterns of the other.

Common Stages of Acculturation of English Language Learners (ELLs)

Euphoria/Honeymoon:	Students experience excitement about being in the new environment. Excitement about all that is new. They are enthusiastic about learning.
Culture Shock (withdrawal/rejection):	Students experience the intrusion of the new culture. Depression, irritability, and difficulty in adjustment may occur. Students feel overwhelmed. They may appear sleepy in class and they might lose interest in learning.
Recovery/Adjustment:	Students experience acceptance or recovery from the initial culture shock. Language proficiency increases and students feel more confident. They show signs of actively adapting to new culture and language challenges. Students tend to link home and new culture. They want to participate in both.
Acceptance/Integration:	Students experience adaptation, assimilation, and ***integration*** of the new culture with renewed self-confidence. They show active and successful participation in the classroom.

Awareness and Respect for Others – Multicultural Community

Stereotyping, *racism*, *ethnocentrism*, *prejudice*, and *discrimination* are social issues that sometimes are difficult to address in the classroom. However, teachers' awareness of personal, social, and cultural differences of their bilingual students will help them understand their students' behaviors and cultures and make the best educational decisions.

Through cooperative activities in the classroom that focus on positive experiences with many different cultures, students can develop appreciation, respect and pride for their own and other cultures [e.g., celebrations of all cultures, guest speakers, cooperative learning (heterogeneous groups), and cultural projects].

Family and Community Involvement

ESL and bilingual teachers are constantly fostering positive cultural involvement inside and outside the classroom by:

1. Building partnerships with parents to continue cognitive development in the first language at home.
2. Inviting ethnic community members to the classroom.
3. Developing multicultural events at school.
4. Providing family literacy programs on weekends or evenings.
5. Asking parents of bilingual students to serve as parent members of school based committees.

ESL and bilingual teachers make sure that school personnel, teachers, students, parents, and members of the community know the advantages of bilingualism:

6. Bilingualism promotes **cognitive** development and **metalinguistic** awareness. Bilinguals develop the knowledge and the ability to consciously manipulate and access linguistic structures. They learn to think and understand how the first language and the second language are similar and different.
7. Bilingualism promotes school achievement. Students develop **literacy** and **biliteracy** by transferring and enriching skills and strategies they learn in their first language to the second language.

8. Bilingualism promotes **cross-cultural awareness** and understanding. Students experience appreciation, value, and respect for cultural and linguistic diversity.
9. Bilingualism promotes communication with the extended family. Bilingual students develop the ability to **bridge** the **generation gap**.
10. Bilingualism promotes potential **economic opportunities** in a more diverse, multicultural global society.

> One language sets you in a corridor for life. Two languages open every door along the way."
> — Frank Smith, Psycholinguist

Competency 10

This content area to be tested is aligned to a set of competencies that correspond to state curriculum guideline standards, curriculum materials, and research-based theoretical and applied second language acquisition subjects.

010 - (I) INVOLVEMENT: The ESL teacher knows how to serve as an advocate for ESL students and facilitate family and community involvement in their education.

The beginning ESL teacher:

A. Applies knowledge of effective strategies advocating educational and social equity for ESL students (e.g., participating in LPAC and Admission, Review and Dismissal (ARD) meetings, serving on Site-Based Decision making (SBDM) committees, serving as a resource for teachers).

B. Understands the importance of family involvement in the education of ESL students and knows how to facilitate parent/guardian participation in their children's education and school activities.

C. Applies skills for communicating and collaborating effectively with the parents/guardians of ESL students in a variety of educational contexts.

D. Knows how community members and resources can positively affect student learning in the ESL program and is able to access community resources to enhance the education of ESL students.

Source: 154 English as a Second Language Supplemental Preparation Manual
Texas Education Agency – www.texes.ets.org

Key Terms/Topics

Participation in Language Proficiency Assessment Committee (LPAC) meetings
Participation in the Admission, Review and Dismissal (ARD) meetings
Participation in Site-Based Decision making (SBDM) committees
Effective communication with parents/guardians
Access community resources to enhance ESL students' education

NOTES

Participation, Roles, Responsibilities

As a representative of ESL education, ESL teachers should be a part of site based decision making committees, LPACs, ARDs, and serve in a role to be a voice for ESL students.

Language Proficiency Assessment Committee (LPAC) – This committee determines identification, placement, and exit of English language learners.

Admission, Review and Dismissal (ARD) - This committee determines identification, placement and exit of special education students.

Site-Based Decision Making Committee (SBDM) – this committee plans strategies and reviews policies for better student achievement each year.

Regulations for school districts:

Each school district in Texas required to offer bilingual education and English a s a second language (ESL) programs shall establish a *Language Proficient Assessment Committee* (LPAC). LPAC committee's members shall be acting for the school district and shall observe regulations governing confidentiality of English language learners. Districts shall be responsible for the orientation and trainings of all LPAC members.

Home Language Survey (HLS):

An HLS is required for every new student to Texas schools. If the HLS indicates that English is spoken at home, and by the student most of the time, no testing is required. If any response to the HLS indicates a **language other than English; spoken at home or by the student, most of the time**, the student must be tested.

Student testing prior ELL classification:

- PreK-1st = Oral Language Proficiency Test (OLPT)
- 2nd-12th = OLPT + Norm Referenced Standardized Achievement Test (NRT)
  - Districts that provide bilingual education must administer the OLPT in English and Spanish. School districts that provide bilingual education in languages other than Spanish, they may use informal oral assessments instruments.
  - Trained professionals or paraprofessionals must administer tests.
  - Both tests (OLPT and NRT) must be Texas Education Agency (TEA) approved tests.

Language Proficiency Assessment Committees (LPACs)

Texas school districts should have policies and procedures for the selection, appointment, and training of members of the *Language Proficiency Assessment Committee* (LPAC).

WHAT	WHO	WHEN THEY MEET	WHY
School districts required to provide a bilingual education or an ESL program. **For school districts and grade levels not required to provide bilingual education, a bilingual teacher is excused.*	-A campus administrator -A professional bilingual educator -An ESL teacher/professional transitional language educator -A parent of a current ELL participating in the current bilingual or ESL program. This parent may not be an employee of the school district. All members must be present.	Upon students' initial enrollment, within **20 school days** of the enrollment of ELLs.	**Classify** students as ELLs. **Designate** the language proficiency level of each ELL. **Designate** the level of academic achievement of each ELL. **Designate**, subject to parental approval, the initial instructional placement of each ELL. **Notify** parents about ELL classification and **request** their permission for program placement. **Provide** parents a description and the benefits of the program. **Facilitate** the participation of ELLs in other special programs.
		Before the administration of the state-criterion referenced test each year.	**Determine** the appropriate assessment option for each ELL.
		At the end of the school year.	**Classify** students as English proficient and **recommend** their exit from the bilingual education or English as a second language program. **Monitor** the academic progress of each student who has exited the bilingual education or ESL program, during the **first 2 years** after exiting the program.

Source: *Adapted from: http://ritter.tea.state.tx.us/rules/tac/chapter089/ch089bb.html"*

Family and Community Involvement

Teachers who work with English language learners (ELLs) need **to facilitate** family and community involvement in their education, and **to access** community resources for parents of ELLs, and school-related community members.

Suggestions for Home-School-Community Relationships:

Building partnerships with parents to continue cognitive development in the first language at home.

Inviting ethnic community members to the classroom.

Developing multicultural events at school.

Providing family literacy programs on weekends or evenings.

Asking parents of ESL students to serve as parent members of school based committees.

Developing home/school communication in a language that parents will understand and by seeking out help if you are not able to speak or write in their language.

REFERENCES

Adamson, H. D. 1993. Academic Competence. Theory and Classroom Practice: Preparing ESL Students for Content Courses. New York: Longman

Baker, C. 1993. Foundations of Bilingual Education and Bilingualism. Clevedon: Multilingual Matters Ltd.

Baker, C. 2007. A Parent' and Teachers' Guide to Bilingualism. Third Edition. Multilingual Matters Ltd.

Baker, C. 2007. Foundations of Bilingual Education and Bilingualism, - Fourth Edition. Clevedon: Multilingual Matters Ltd.

Beeman, K., & Urow Cheryl. 2013. Teaching for Biliteracy – Strengthening Bridges between Languages. Caslon Publishing, Philadelphia.

Brown, H.D. 1987. Principles of Language learning and Teaching. New Jersey: Englewood Cliffs.

Brown, H.D. 2007. Teaching by Principles – An interactive Approach to language Pedagogy. Pearson Education, Inc.

Collier, V. 1995. Promoting Academic Success for ESL Students. Understanding Second Language Acquisition for School. New Jersey: NJTESOL-BE

Cummins, J. 1979. Cognitive/Academic Language Proficiency, linguistic interdependence, the optimal age question and other matters. Working Papers on Bilingualism 19:197-205.

Cummins, J. 1989b. Language Proficiency and Academic Achievement. In J. Cummins & M. Swain, Bilingualism in Education (pp. 138-161). New York: Longman

Carrasquillo, A., & Rodríguez, V. 1996. Language Minority Students in the Mainstream Classroom. Clevedon: Multilingual Matters.

Chamot, A., & O'Malley, J.M. 1994. The CALLA Handbook. Implementing the Cognitive Academic Language Learning Approach. New York: Addison-Wesley Publishing Company.

Chang, K. Chen, I., & Sung, Y. 2002. The effect of concept mapping to enhance text comprehension and summarization. *The Journal of Experimental Education 71*(1), 5-23.

Chomsky, N. 1964. Current Issues in Linguistic Theory. In Fodor and Katz 1964.

Crawford J. (1995) Bilingual Education: History Politics Theiry and Practice. Third Edition. Bilingual Education Services, Inc.

Dalbor B. J. (1980). Spanish Pronunciation. Theory and Practice. Second Edition. Holt, Rinehart and Winston, Inc.

Echeverria, J., Vogt, M., & Short D. 2008. Making Content Comprehensible for English Language Learners – The SIOP Model, Pearson Education Inc.

Echeverria, J., Vogt, M., & Short D. 2008. Response to Intervention (RTI) and English Learners. Making It Happen– The SIOP Model, Pearson Education Inc.

Escamilla, K. 1999. Teaching Literacy in Spanish. In Devilla, R., & Tinajero, J. The Power of Two Languages. 2000. New York: McMillan/McGraw Hill, 126-141.

Escamilla J., Hopewell, S., S., & Sparrow, W. 2014. Biliteracy from the Start. Caslon Publishing, Philadelphia.

Fasold R., & Connor-Linton, J. (2006) An Introduction to Language and Linguistics. Cambridge University Press.

Farrell T., 2006. Succeeding with English Language Learners – A Guide for Beginning Teachers. Corwin Press.

Finocchiaro, Mary 1989. English as a Second/Foreign Language: From Theory to Practice. New Jersey: Englewood Cliffs

Fishman, J. 1972. Language and Nationalism. Rowley, MA: Newbury House.

Fodor, J. & Katz J. 1964 The Structure of Language Readings in the Philosophy of Language. Englewood Cliff, NJ: Prentice-Hall.

Freeman, Y., & Freeman, D. 1992. Whole Language for Second Language Learners. Heinemann Portsmouth, NH.

Freeman, Y., & Freeman, D. 1996. Teaching Reading and Writing in the Spanish Bilingual Classroom. Heineman, Porstmouth, NH

Freeman, Y., & Freeman, D. 2001 Between Worlds – Access to Second Language Acquisition. Heinemann Portsmouth, NH.

Freeman, Y., Freeman, D., & Ramírez R., 2008 Diverse Learners in the Mainstream Classroom. Heinemann Portsmouth, NH.

Freeman, Y., & Freeman, D. 1992. Whole Language for Second Language Learners. Heinemann Portsmouth, NH.

Gardner, R., & Lambert, W. 1975. Attitudes and Motivation in Second Language Learning. Rowley, MA: Newbury House Publishers.

Gattegno, C. 1972. Teaching Foreign Languages in School: The Silent Way. Second Edition. New York: Educational Solutions.

Grady, W., Archibald, J., Aronoff, A., & Rees-Miller, J. 2001. Contemporary Linguistics. Bedford/St. Martin's.

Gottlieb, M. 2006. Assessing English Language Learners – *Bridges from Language Proficiency to Academic Achievement*. Corwin Press.

Goodman, K. 1970. Reading: A psycholinguistic Guessing Game. In Singer and Ruddell 1970.

Halliday, M. 1973. Explorations in the Function of Language. London: Edward Arnold.

Hornberger, N. 2003. Continua of Biliteracy. An Ecological Framework for Educational Policy, Research, and Practice in Multilingual Setting. Multilingual Matters Ltd.

Hamayan, E., Genesee, F., & Cloud N. 2013. Dual Language Instruction. Heinemann, Portsmouth, NH.

Kottler, E., Kottler J, & Street C. 2008. English Language Learners in Your Classroom – Strategies that Work. Corwin Press.

Krashen, S., & Terrel, T. 1983. The Natural Approach: Language Acquisition in the Classroom. Oxford: Pergamon Press.

Krashen, S. 1992. Fundamentals of Language Education. Torrance: Laredo Publishing Co., Inc.

Law, B., & Eckes M.1995. Assessment and ESL. A handbook for K-12 Teachers, Peguis Publishers Ltda.

Law, B. & Eckes, M. 2000. The More than Just Surviving Handbook. ESL for Every Classroom Teacher. Winnipeg: Portage & Main Press.

Lehr, F., Osborn, J., & Hiebert, F. 2005. Research Based Practices in Reading. A Focus on Comprehension. Pacific Resources for Education and Learning.

Lozanov, G. 1979. Suggestology and Outlines of Suggestopedy. New York: Gordon and Breach Science Publishers.

Mora-Flores, E. 2013. Connecting Content and Language. Shell Education.

Martin-Jones, M., & Jones, K. 2000. Introduction: Multilingual Literacies. In Martin-Jones & K. Jones. Multilingual Differences: Reading /Writing in Different Worlds. Amsterdam/Philadelphia: John Benjamins.

Morales, P. 2016. Content Review and Practice Book for the Texas Educator Certification Program. 164 Bilingual Education Supplemental. First Edition. Ell services.

O'Malley, J., & Chamot, A. 1990. Learning Strategies in Second Language Acquisition. Cambridge: Cambridge University Press.

Raymond, E. 2000. Cognitive Characteristics. *Learners with Mild Disabilities* (pp. 169-201). Needham Heights, MA: Allyn & Bacon. Pearson Education Inc.

Richard –Amato, P., & Snow, M. 2005. Academic Success for English Language Learners. Longman.

Rodríguez, D., Carrasquillo, A., & Soon Lee, K. 2014. The Bilingual Advantage. Teachers College. Columbia University. New York and London.

Saville-Troike, M. 1997. What really matters in second language learning for academic purposes? TESOL Quarterly, 18(2), 199-219.

Saville-Troike, M. 2012. Introducing Second Language Acquisition. Cambridge University Press.

Singer, H., & Ruddell, R. 1970. Toward an Analysis of Discourse. The English Used by Teachers and Pupils. Oxford: Oxford University Press.

Skinner, B. F. 1957. Verbal Behavior. New York: Appleton Century Crofts.

Spangenberg-Urbschat, K., & Pritchard, R. 1994. Kids Come in All Languages: Reading Instruction for ESL Students. Delaware: International Reading Association.

Sousa, D. 2011. How the ELL Brain Learns. Corwin Press.

Stanley Whitley M. 1986. Spanish/English Contrasts. Georgetown University Press, Washinton, D.C.

Valdés-Fallis, G. 1987. Languages in Education Series, No 4: Code-Switching and the Classroom Teacher. Arlington, VA: Center for Applied Linguistics.

Wells, G & G. Chang-Wells. 1992. Constructing Knowledge Together. Portsmouth, NH: Heinemann.

Whorf, B. 1956. Science and Linguistics. In Carroll 1956.

PRACTICE QUESTIONS

Competency 001

1. Use the following writing sample to answer the question below.

I goed to the house of Claudia with my mother. She drived her car.

Based on the writing sample, the student needs practice on:

A. Subject-Verb agreement
B. Position of the subject pronoun
C. Use of irregular verbs
D. Syntax

2. Read the words below.

piece	***peace***
eye	***I***
right	***write***

The pair of words in each row has the same pronunciation but differ in meaning. They are:

A. Synonyms
B. Antonyms
C. Homophones
D. Allophones

3. How many phonemes does the word ***sunny*** contain?

A. Five
B. Three allophones
C. This word does not contain phonemes
D. Four

Competency 002

4. Ms. Flores makes sure all students in her class understand the content. To facilitate communication, she repeats and paraphrases key words, ideas, making clear the meaning in context. Ms. Flores's teaching strategy is based on which Second Language Acquisition hypothesis:

A. Threshold hypothesis
B. Comprehensible input hypothesis
C. Monitor hypothesis
D. Affective Filter hypothesis

5. Mrs. Brown, the school superintendent, visited Mr. Garrison's ESL class. As Mrs. Brown entered the room, several English language learners greeted her by saying: "Hey, what's up girl". Mr. Garrison apologized to the superintendent and decided to plan a lesson on:

A. Affection
B. Morphology
C. Syntax
D. Pragmatics

6. This theory states that individuals are born with a universal grammar wired into their brain, which they use as a pattern for language acquisition. Human beings have an innate capacity for language. This description corresponds to which of the following theories in language acquisition.

A. The Behavioristic Approach
B. The Nativist Approach
C. The Functional Approach
D. The Structural Approach

7. Current theories of cognitive bilingualism state that *...irrespective of the language a person is operating, the thoughts that accompany speaking, listening, reading and writing come from the same central engine. When a person owns two or more languages, there is an integrated source of thought...* This theory is known as:

A. The Threshold Hypothesis
B. The Monitor Hypothesis
C. The Common Underlying Proficiency (CUP) Hypothesis
D. The Acquisition Learning Hypothesis

8. A beginning English language learner wrote the following:

"I visited the house red with grandparents mine" The student's arrangement of words in the sentence below shows which of the following:

A. Code switching from L1
B. Incorrect use of allophones from L1
C. Syntactical interference from L1
D. Phonological interference from L1

9. According to research, most English language learners take an average of five to seven years to develop:

A. Cognitive academic language proficiency
B. Social-communicative competence
C. Syntactic and lexical accuracy
D. Pragmatic school expression

Competency 003

10. Ms. Murillo, an ESL teacher, asks her students to do a research project on the causes of the Civil War, the state populations at that time, and the number of soldiers involved. This project relates to the content students are covering in social studies, language arts, and mathematics. Which of the following is the strategy that Ms. Murillo is trying to develop?

A. A Natural Way Approach
B. A Total Physical Response Approach
C. An Interdisciplinary/Integrative Instructional Approach
D. A Suggestopedia/Integrative Approach

11. This methodology focuses on teaching oral and written communicative skills based on the theoretical assumption that English language learners develop language through meaningful interaction, low anxiety classroom atmosphere, and enough comprehensible input. This ESL approach is known as:

A. Total Physical Response
B. The CALLA Approach
C. The Natural Approach
D. The Silent Way

12. This approach is based on theories from structural linguistics and behavioral psychology. Memorization, mimicry and manipulation drills are its essential features.

A. The Cognitive Approach
B. The Audiolingual Method
C. The Direct Method
D. The Natural Approach

13. Mrs. Rosenberg, an ESL teacher, has a population of English language learners mostly composed of beginners. She is trying to promote among her students the comprehension of simple present tense verbs through daily actions. She says: - "I get up at 6", and acts out the verb, and then she asks her students to imitate her action verbs. Which instructional method is Mrs. Rosenberg developing?

A. Suggestopedia
B. Silent Way
C. Total Physical Response
D. Functional Syllabus

Competency 004

14. Lee is a recent arrival and he's been placed in a sheltered class. During class he remains quiet and is hesitant to participate orally and tends to use non-verbal communication to function in English. Lee is acquiring communicative competence through which of the following stages?

A. Intermediate stage
B. Early Production stage
C. Pre-Production stage
D. Affective Filter stage

15. Which of the following instructional practices would best promote the oral language development of beginning English language learners?

A. The focus should be on language content or functions rather than grammatical form.
B. Providing English language learners with individualized instruction that allows them to complete their work independently.
C. Using context-reduced language and paraphrasing during instruction to facilitate the transfer of concepts form L1 to English.
D. Providing English language learners with teacher-guided instruction to facilitate students' development of content vocabulary words in written sentences.

16. During this oral development stage, English language learners use short sentences and make attempts to communicate complete thoughts. Students have a vocabulary of 3,000 words and communicate with simple phrases and sentences. This stage is known as:

A. The Telegraphic stage
B. The Social/Academic Competence stage
C. The Oral Developmental stage
D. The Speech Emergence stage

17. The four language skills (listening, speaking, reading, and writing) are divided in which of the following categories:

A. Productive and Affective skills
B. Expressive and Productive skills
C. Receptive and Expressive skills
D. Affective and Receptive skills

18. Previous knowledge, learning strategies, social competence, and degree of first language proficiency are best described as:

A. Social/Cultural student differences
B. Individual/Intrapersonal student differences
C. Interpersonal/Social student differences
D. Informal/Interpersonal student difference.

Competency 005

19. Mrs. Boyd was in charge of collecting writing samples from her English language learners to comply with the *Texas English Language Proficiency Assessment System* (TELPAS). Mrs. Boyd noticed that one writing sample by a first-year English language learner contained several Vietnamese words in the English sentences. The sample was characterized by which of the following:

A. Assimilation
B. Acculturation
C. Code Switching
D. Diglossia

20. Which of the following describes the ability to recognize the sounds of spoken language and how these sounds can be manipulated, segmented, and blended together?

A. Fluency of sounds
B. Alphabetic principle
C. Phonological awareness
D. Syntactical development

21. Mrs. Pellegrini has five English language learners from Argentina. All of them are at the beginning level of English acquisition; however they have been transferring literacy skills from their first language during the year they have been in her reading class. In order to prepare a lesson in narrative writing, Mrs. Pellegrini plans to read a portion of a text aloud and ask her students to present a brief oral speech containing the main points of the paragraph. Which strategy would best help her students transfer their literacy skills from Spanish into English?

A. Ask students to select a similar paragraph and write a comparison in Spanish.
B. Ask students to bring illustrations from their homes to add to the written report in Spanish.
C. Ask students to summarize the paragraph in Spanish and then transcribe the summary to English.
D. Ask students to compile unfamiliar words from the text and make a list for further reference.

22. An ESL teacher is trying to promote free writing among her ESL students who are at the beginning level of English proficiency. What is the best strategy she should use?

A. Ask students to write in English only because they need to use their second language.
B. Ask students to write in English or in their first language to express their ideas and emotions.
C. Ask students to write sentences in English to express their experiences.
D. Ask students to collaborate with their peers.

23. Which of the following situations illustrates phonological interference of literacy competency from L1 to L2?

A. An English language learner is not able to understand English idioms.
B. An English language learner applies letter-sound association from her/his first language to English.
C. An English language learner is not able to comprehend formal discourse in English.
D. An English learner is not able to arrange words appropriately in an English sentences.

24. Jeong is at the intermediate level in reading development according to scores from the Texas English Language Proficiency Assessment System (TELPAS). She is originally from Korea and her parents approved her placement in the ESL program two years ago. Jeong's oral competency is progressing due to the fact that she participates frequently in group activities with ample opportunities for social interaction. However, her fluency levels in reading are low. Which of the following strategies would be most effective in helping Jeong improve her reading fluency?

A. Encourage Jeong to use prior knowledge to understand meaning in English.
B. Give Jeong frequent opportunities to read stories at her independent reading level.
C. Assign Jeong a buddy for assistance.
D. Make sure Jeong use self-monitoring and predicting techniques.

25. A fourth-grade class includes a number of English language learners who are at the pre-production stage of English acquisition. When compiling reading materials for those students, the ESL teacher should select materials that.

A. Attract students' interest and promote their predicting skills through academic words.
B. Include meaningful illustrations and high-frequency words.
C. Model a variety of different writing styles.
D. Focus on academic vocabulary in content.

Competency 006

26. A group of sixth-grade ESL students is developing a semantic map in social studies. They are using a dictionary in English and Spanish as supplemental material to develop the map. One student points to one of the words, and says "ejecutivo". Executive in English and ejecutivo in Spanish is an example of:

A. Idiomatic expressions
B. Cultural expressions
C. Cognates
D. Morphemes

27. Abdul, a third grader speaks English well after being in an ESL program for two years. His parents requested that he be placed in a mainstream classroom this school year. Abdul's oral competence is fine but he is having difficulty comprehending the science textbook. What might explain this?

A. He has developed oral competency only and he needs to develop academic vocabulary.
B. He needs to be involved in cooperative learning activities to improve social competence.
C. Parents need to be more involved in Abdul's learning process.
D. Teachers are not giving Abdul the opportunity to work independently.

28. Mrs. Ryan facilitates beginning English language learners' internalization of new linguistic structures and academic concepts in science by developing among her English language learners strategies such as self-talk, questioning for clarification and cooperation. These strategies are best described as:

A. Metacognitive strategies
B. Cognitive strategies
C. Social/Affective strategies
D. Competence strategies

29. Which of the following statements best describes the features of a Venn diagram?

A. Students are able to compare and contrast.
B. Students are able to organize in a sequence.
C. Students are able to produce a series of connected events.
D. Students are able to connect themes with several categories.

Competency 007

30. A middle school teacher tells the ESL teacher that one of her students who is an English language learner has not performed well on the Texas English Language Proficiency Assessment System (TELPAS). The ESL teacher explains to her that:

A. ESL student may retake the assessment for three years until they pass.
B. The TELPAS measures students' annual progress of English proficiency and scores should be used for instructional planning.
C. The TELPAS is an optional measure that is designed to help ESL students develop academic proficiency.
D. Students who fail TELPAS need to be monitored for two years until they pass.

31. A math teacher teaches regular algebra and sheltered algebra. For the sheltered class, he is planning content-based instructional strategies based on his students' English proficiency levels. To accomplish his task, he reviews the information that lists the students' English language proficiency levels; beginning, intermediate, advanced, and advanced high. Which instrument is the math teacher reviewing?

A. Standardized Achievement Test (SAT)
B. The Texas Assessment of Academic Readiness (STAAR)
C. The Home Language Survey (HLS)
D. The Texas English Language Proficiency Assessment System (TELPAS)

32. Use the information below to answer the question that follows.

A fifth-grade student arrived from his home country, Ecuador, last year with no prior formal education. He is now in his second year in a Texas school and is receiving bilingual services. He is still at the beginning stages of Spanish literacy development, English language development, and academic development. What would be the most effective way to assess the student's academic competence in science?

A. An assessment in Spanish
B. No assessment
C. An academic assessment in English and/or Spanish with linguistic accommodations
D. An assessment of language proficiency only.

33. Which of the following would be the most appropriate way for evaluating the linguistic progress of English language learners who are at different proficiency levels in English?

A. Using samples of daily work, observations, and student portfolios.
B. Using norm-referenced tests and compile data for instructional planning and student achievement.
C. Using criterion-referenced tests to establish a grading curve.
D. Using standardized achievement tests and ability tests to compare and contrast.

34. A science teacher is teaching "forms of energy" to English language learners. He is very careful when planning a way of assessing students' content knowledge. He makes sure that the content of the test matches the content domain associated with the construct, which is "forms of energy". Which assessment concept is the teacher addressing?

A. Fairness
B. Equity
C. Cultural Bias
D. Validity

Competency 008

35. Nichols ISD has a student population of 3 English language learners in second grade, 6 in first grade, 18 in fourth grade, and 2 at the kindergarten level. Which program is required for this population of students?

A. English as a Second Language
B. Bilingual Education or English as a Second Language
C. Bilingual Education only
D. Dual language instruction only

36. Mr. and Mrs. Gómez have decided to take their son out of the ESL program due to the fact that he is being pulled out from the science class to receive ESL instruction. Ms. Brown, the science teacher just received her ESL endorsement. What should the principal do?

A. Ask the parents to sign a parental denial form as soon as possible.
B. Keep the student in the science class because the science teacher is ESL certified.
C. Invite the student's parents to attend ESL classes in the evenings.
D. Encourage parents to talk with the counselor.

37. A Texas high school develops special services for English language learners who are at beginning levels of English proficiency, by providing personalized instruction. It is their goal that they experience success when they return to their home schools. Students generally stay with them for one or two semesters. This program is known as:

A. Structural Submersion
B. Dual Language
C. Newcomer Program
D. ESL Pull-Out

38. This Supreme Court rules that identical education does not constitute equal education under the Civil Rights Act. This case is known as:

A. Bilingual Education Act
B. Similar Opportunity Act
C. Lau vs. Nichols
D. Plyler vs. Doe

39. Mr. and Mrs. Chang have a 5-year-old son named Lue. They only speak Chinese and would like to enroll their son in the English/Chinese Bilingual Education program so he can maintain and develop academic Chinese which is his native language. What would be the best choice for Lue?

A. Be placed in a pull-out program.
B. Be placed in a two-way dual language program.
C. Be placed in a self-contained ESL program with sheltered instruction.
D. Be placed in an alternative ESL program for newcomers.

40. In which court case was it stipulated that undocumented students could not be excluded from public schools?

A. Lau vs. Nichols
B. Civil Rights Act
C. Bilingual Education Act
D. Plyler vs. Doe

41. Which of the following descriptions best characterizes the instruction of English language learners in the United States between the 1920´s and 1960´s?

A. Most of the students' population attended private schools.
B. English proficiency was part of the student curriculum.
C. Students were placed in remedial classes.
D. The method of instruction was known as "sink or swim."

42. A ninth-grade student was tested at the beginning of the school year for program eligibility purposes. He scored fluent on the English language proficiency test (OLPT), and scored 65th percentile on the achievement test used by the district. According to Texas regulations, what program placement should the LPAC recommend for this student?

A. Bilingual Education
B. ESL Instruction
C. All-English classroom
D. ESL Instruction and Special Education

Competency 009

43. During this stage of acculturation, English language learners experience the intrusion of the new culture. They may appear sleepy in class and they might lose interest in learning. Some students feel overwhelmed and depressed. This stage is known as:

A. The Awareness stage
B. The Adjustment stage
C. The Culture Shock stage
D. The Euphoria stage

44. During an informal conversation with the science teacher, a fifth grade English language learner, mentioned he was not interested in using his first language in the classroom. He mentioned he is embarrassed to go shopping with his parents because they can't speak English. What should the Science teacher do?

A. Ask the student's parents to try to communicate in English when they go shopping with their son.
B. Organize students in small groups and ask them to develop a research project about the positive benefits of being bilingual.
C. Try to use as much as English as possible in the class to help all students develop English rapidly.
D. Ask the student's parents to attend the ESL classes in the evenings.

45. The members of a group or a culture are absorbed into a culture and lose characteristics of the first culture. Most of the time, the members of the group are forced to accept the new culture and give up their original culture. This process is known as:

A. Adaptation
B. Acculturation
C. Assimilation
D. Affective Filter

46. Based on current demographic research, the population of English language learners is increasing at a very fast rate. There are over hundred and twenty languages spoken in our Texas school districts. Based on this information an effective ESL teacher should:

A. Know how to promote bilingual education and satisfy the affective, linguistic, and cognitive needs of diverse populations.
B. Know how to create an effective multicultural and multilingual learning environment that addresses the different needs of ESL students.
C. Know how to promote English as a second language through effective pull-out programs.
D. Know how to integrate technological tools and resources into the instructional process to facilitate English linguistic development.

Competency 010

47. Mr. and Mrs. Guerrero's daughter qualifies for the bilingual program. They don't want her to be in the bilingual program because they think that the time spent learning in Spanish will detract her from learning English. As a member of the Language Proficiency Assessment Committee (LPAC), what information would you share with the parents?

A. You would tell them they need to sign a program denial before the end of the school year.
B. You would tell them that in the bilingual program the student develops grade-level content as well as English acquisition.
C. You would ask their approval to place the student in regular education.
D. You would invite them to attend parent's ESL classes on Saturdays.

48. A student who was in the ESL program for three years, met the state exit requirements and was placed in an all-English classroom. A year later, the Language Proficiency Assessment Committee (LPAC) realized the student was not doing well in social studies. What should the members of the LPAC committee do?

A. The LPAC committee should monitor the student for two years after they realized he was failing social studies.
B. The LPAC committee should talk to the student's parents as soon as possible.
C. The LPAC committee should recommend after school tutorials or any other extra support program in social studies after they review the student's specific academic needs.
D. The LPAC committee should develop a detailed list of modifications to help the student improve linguistic needs and oral proficiency in English.

49. According to the Texas Commissioner's Rules for Special Populations, Sub Chapter BB, what is the Language Proficiency Assessment Committee (LPAC) primary responsibility?

A. Assess linguistic proficiency in the second language and in the primary language
B. Designate language proficiency, level of academic achievement, and recommend program placement, subject to parents' approval.
C. Administer oral language proficiency tests in English and Spanish, and facilitate the participation of English language learners in other special programs
D. Classify students as English proficient in accordance with district and state polici

50. In districts required to offer a bilingual program, the Language Proficiency Assessment Committee (LPAC) should be composed by:

A. A professional bilingual educator and a parent of an English language learner.
B. A parent of an ELL, a campus administrator, and a bilingual teacher.
C. A campus administrator and an ESL teacher.
D. An ESL teacher, a professional bilingual educator, and a parent of an English language learner.

Answer Key and Rationales

Question Number	Competency Number	Correct Answer	Rationales
1	1	C	Option **C** is correct because the student needs practice on the use of **irregular verbs**. The student is overgeneralizing the simple past tense –suffix *ed*. Option A is incorrect because there is an agreement between the subject and the verb. Option B is incorrect because the subject pronoun *I* is in the right position, at the beginning of the sentence. Option D is incorrect because semantics has to do with meaning, and the question is related to syntax.
2	1	C	Option **C** is correct because **homophones** have the same pronunciation but different meaning. Option A is incorrect because synonyms are words that have different spelling but similar meaning. Option B is incorrect because antonyms are words that have different spelling and different meaning. Option D is incorrect because allophones are sounds that may occur in a particular phonetic environment (part of a word); such as at the beginning of a word, middle of the word, or at the end of the word.
3	1	D	Option **D** is correct because **phonemes** are the sounds the word contains not the letters. Sunny contains 4 phonemes (sounds; /s/ /ʌ/ /n/ /i/) and 5 graphemes (letters; *sunny*). Option A is incorrect because the phonemes are 4 not 5. Option B is incorrect because the question is about the number of phonemes the word contains. Option C is incorrect because the word contains phonemes (sounds).
4	2	B	Option **B** is correct because the teacher is making content comprehensible to students by repeating and paraphrasing key words and ideas, which is the philosophy behind the Comprehensible Input Hypothesis. Option A is incorrect because the Threshold Hypothesis has to do with the relationship between cognition and degree of Bilingualism. Option C is incorrect because the Monitor Hypothesis refers to the editing device the learner uses to monitor himself/herself. Option D is incorrect because the Affective Filter Hypothesis has to do with the affective elements (anxiety, frustration, etc.) that may affect the process of learning a second language.
5	2	D	Option **D** is correct because Ms. Brown needs to teach the difference between **formal and informal registers** which is part of pragmatics. Option A is incorrect because the question does not focus on affection (affective elements: anxiety, fear,…). Option B is incorrect because the question does not focus on morphology (formation of words). Option C is incorrect because the question does not focus on syntax (sentence structure).
6	2	B	Option **B** is correct because the description corresponds to the **Nativist Approach**. Option A is incorrect because the Behavioristic Approach does not correspond to the definition of the question. Option C is incorrect because the Functional Approach does not correspond to the definition of the question. Option D is incorrect because the Nativist Approach was against Structural Linguistics.
7	2	C	Option **C** is correct. The **CUP model** states that when a person is proficient in two languages, experience, knowledge, and thoughts transfer from one language to another. Option A, B, and D do not correspond to the definition stated in the question.

Question Number	Competency Number	Correct Answer	Rationales
8	2	C	Option **C** is correct because the ELL is imposing his/her L1 **syntax** when writing in English. Option A is incorrect because the student is not inserting L1 words in the sentence. Option B is incorrect because the question has nothing to do with allophones (sounds). Option D is incorrect because there is no evidence of phonological (sound) interference.
9	2	A	Option **A** is correct because ELLs take an average of 5 to 7 years to develop **Cognitive Academic Language Proficiency (CALP)**. Option B is incorrect because social communicative competence is acquired in the first two years of being exposed to a second language. Option C is incorrect because the questions has nothing to do with syntactic (sentence structure) and lexical (vocabulary) accuracy. Option D is incorrect because the question is not related to the use of language in social context (pragmatics).
10	3	C	Option **C** is correct because the ESL teacher is integrating the ESL content across different subject areas. Option A is incorrect because the Natural Approach is a language approach based on natural language acquisition. Option B is incorrect because the Total Physical Response is a kinesthetic approach useful for beginners. Option D is incorrect because the Suggestopedia Approach is a language method that is based on the idea that learners can process language if they are given a condition such as relaxation.
11	3	C	Option **C** is correct. The description of the methodology corresponds to the **Natural Approach**. Options A, B, and D do not correspond to the definition stated in the question.
12	3	B	Option **B** is correct. The description of the method corresponds to the **Audiolingual method**. Options A, C, and D do not correspond to the definition stated in the question.
13	3	C	Option **C** is correct. The teacher is teaching ESL through a **Kinesthetic Approach** known as the Total Physical Response (TPR). Options A, B and D do not represent the methodology used in the example.
14	4	C	Option **C** is correct because a student is going through a Silent period and also called **Pre-Production stage**. He is not ready to produce verbal speech yet. Option A is incorrect because during the Intermediate Fluency stage the student communicates through short sentences. Option B is incorrect because during the Early Production stage the student produces one or two word utterances. Option D is incorrect because the Affective Filter is not an oral development stage.
15	4	A	Option **A** is correct because ELLs at the beginning levels need to develop language naturally. Emphasis should be placed on function rather than grammar. Option B is incorrect because independent work does not improve oral development, interaction with others do. Option C is incorrect because context-reduced language does not provide context clues (visuals, videos, real objects, etc.) to facilitate understanding. Option D is incorrect because the development of written vocabulary does not contribute to oral development.
16	4	D	Option **D** is correct because the description corresponds to the **Speech Emergence stage**. Options A, B, and C do not correspond to the definition of the Speech Emergence stage.

Question Number	Competency Number	Correct Answer	Rationales
17	4	C	Option **C** is correct because listening and reading are **Receptive Skills** and speaking and writing are Productive or Expressive Skills. Option A and D are incorrect because listening and reading skills are language skills not affective skills. Option B is incorrect because expressive and productive skills refer to the same language skills; speaking and writing only.
18	4	B	Option **B** is correct because the question asks about individual or intrapersonal differences. Option A is incorrect because the definition in the question is not related to social differences. Option C is incorrect because the definition relates to individual differences only. Option D is incorrect because the question is not related to informality.
19	5	C	Option **C** is correct because the student was inserting L1 words in English sentences. Option A is incorrect because the example is not related to the process of cultural assimilation. Option B is incorrect because the question is not related to the process of acculturation. Option D is incorrect because the question is not related to Diglossia (two languages used by a single community or society).
20	5	C	Option **C** is correct because the description corresponds to **Phonological Awareness**; one of the first reading skills to develop. Option A is incorrect because fluency includes rate, accuracy and prosody when reading, and the question focuses on awareness of sounds only. Option B is incorrect because the alphabetic principle refers to the correspondence between letters and sounds. Option D is incorrect because the question is not related to syntax.
21	5	C	Option **C** is correct because summarizing a paragraph is a **cognitive literacy skill** that transfers to another language. Beginners need to be able to use their L1 resources to have them make sense of the second language and transfer skills. Option A is incorrect because selecting a similar paragraph and writing a comparison in Spanish does not contribute to the transfer of narrative writing. Option B is incorrect because illustrations are not a literacy skill. Option D is incorrect because making a list of unfamiliar words will not help students transfer literacy skills from L1 to English.
22	5	B	Option **B** is correct because beginners will feel more comfortable expressing feelings in L1. Options A and C are incorrect because beginners do not have enough resources to write in English yet. Option D is incorrect because collaboration does not promote free writing.
23	5	B	Option **B** is correct because students will impose their own **Phonological competency** (L1) when reading in English. English language learners apply letter-sound association from their first language to English. Option A is incorrect because idioms are not related to phonological (sound) interference. Idioms correspond to the area of Semantics (meaning). Option C is incorrect because the question is not related to pragmatics (formal discourse). Option D is incorrect because the question is not related to syntax (sentence order).

Question Number	Competency Number	Correct Answer	Rationales
24	5	B	Option **B** is correct because independent reading will help Jeong improve fluency rate. Option A is incorrect because the use of prior knowledge to understand meaning does not help improve fluency rate. Option C is incorrect because a buddy is not going to guarantee improvement on student's fluency rate. Option D is incorrect because predicting and self-monitoring techniques are not going to improve the student's fluency rate.
25	5	B	Option **B** is correct because beginners in the silent period (**Pre-Production stage**) need lots of pictures and high-frequency words to understand new meaning and transfer concepts already learned to their L2. Option A is incorrect because predicting is a metacognitive skill that takes time to transfer. Option C is incorrect because modeling writing styles is not related to materials. Option D is incorrect because academic vocabulary takes longer to be developed and transferred.
26	6	C	Option **C** is correct because the words *ejecutivo* and *executive* are cognates. They are Latin-based, have the same origin and they mean the same. Option A is incorrect because *executive* and *ejecutivo* are not idioms. Option B is incorrect because the question is not related to culture. Option D is incorrect because the question is related to vocabulary words not to parts of a word (morpheme).
27	6	A	Option **A** is correct because the student has not yet developed the academic vocabulary to understand the science book. Option B is incorrect because Abdul's social competence is fine. Option C is incorrect because the question is not related to parent involvement. Option D is incorrect because there is no evidence of not receiving independent work.
28	6	C	Option **C** is correct because the description corresponds to the definition of **Social/Affective strategies**. Options A, B, and D do not correspond to the definition of Social Affective strategies.
29	6	A	Option **A** is correct because the description defines the purpose of a **Venn Diagram**. Options B, C, and D do not correspond to a Venn Diagram.
30	7	B	Option **B** is correct because **TELPAS** scores should be used for instructional purposes. Options A and D are incorrect because TELPAS is not a pass or fail test. Option C is incorrect because TELPAS is not optional.
31	7	D	Option **D** is correct because the assessment instrument is known as **TELPAS**. Option A is incorrect because the definition does not correspond to a Standardized Achievement Test. Option B is incorrect because STAAR measures knowledge and skills and not English proficiency. Option C is incorrect because the Home Language Survey shows the language the student speaks at home.
32	7	C	Option **C** is correct because the student **needs linguistic accommodations** in both languages. Option A is incorrect because the student's level of Spanish literacy is low. Option B is incorrect because the student should receive a valid assessment. Option D is incorrect because the teacher wants to assess the student's academic competence.

Question Number	Competency Number	Correct Answer	Rationales
33	7	A	Option **A** is correct because informal observation of daily work is more appropriate for a **mixed-ability group**. Option B is incorrect because a norm-referenced test is not a valid measure when assessing a mixed-ability group. Option C is incorrect because a criterion-referenced test measures content objectives, not language acquisition. Option D is incorrect because standardized achievement tests are not valid for a mixed ability group.
34	7	D	Option **D** is correct because the validity of a test is the degree to which the test measures what it claims to measure. Options A, B, and C are incorrect because the teacher's purpose is to measure content only. The question is not related to equity or cultural bias.
35	8	A	Option **A** is correct because, based on the demographics, the district is required to offer English as a second language (ESL). Option B and C are incorrect because, based on the number of students, the district is not required to offer bilingual education. Option D is incorrect because Dual Language programs are optional.
36	8	B	Option **B** is correct because the principal should offer the best option available to ELL students. Keeping the student with the ESL Certified teacher is the best instructional setting for the student. Option A is incorrect because a denial is not appropriate. Option C is incorrect because the question is related to the students' best instructional setting, not to the parents' English acquisition. Option D is incorrect because it is the principal's responsibility to offer the student the best instructional setting.
37	8	C	Option **C** is correct because the description corresponds to the **Newcomer program**. Options A, B, and C do not correspond to the definition of a newcomer program.
38	8	C	Option **C** is correct because the description of the court case describes **Lau v. Nichols**. Options A, B, and D do not correspond to the description in the question.
39	8	B	Option **B** is correct because a two-way (English/Chinese) **Dual Language program** will address Lue's L1 and L2 language and academic needs. Option A is incorrect because in a Pull-out program L1 is not used as an instructional language. Option C is incorrect because in a Content-based ESL program, L1 is not used as a language of instruction. Option D is incorrect because in an ESL program the language of instruction is English.
40	8	D	Option **D** is correct because in **Plyler v. Doe**, the Supreme Court denies the state's right to exclude the children of illegal immigrants from public education. Options A, B, and C do not correspond to the description stated in the question.
41	8	D	Option **D** is correct because no language programs were available for language minority groups during that time. Option A is incorrect because there is no evidence to support private school attendance. Option B is incorrect because there were no language programs for English Language Learners. Option C is incorrect because there is no remedial classes for ELLs during those years.

Question Number	Competency Number	Correct Answer	Rationales
42	**8**	**C**	Option **C** is correct because the student does not qualify for ESL or Bilingual services. Options A, B, and D are incorrect because, based on the testing scores, the student does not qualify for any language programs. Therefore, the student should be placed in a mainstream classroom.
43	**9**	**C**	Option **C** is correct because the description corresponds to the **Culture Shock stage**. Options A, B, and D are considered stages of acculturation but do not correspond to the description stated in the question.
44	**9**	**B**	Option **B** is correct because ESL teachers should promote **Bilingualism and Multiculturalism**. Options A and D are incorrect because the question does not focus on parents' communication skills. Option C is incorrect because the progress of a student's English proficiency will not necessarily help the student appreciate the benefit of being bilingual.
45	**9**	**C**	Option **C** is correct because the description defines the concept of **Cultural Assimilation**. Options A, B, and D do not correspond to the definition stated in the question.
46	**9**	**B**	Option **B** is correct because ESL teachers know how to create an effective ESL environment where all languages and cultures are appreciated. Option A is incorrect because an ESL teacher is not qualified to promote bilingual education. Option C is incorrect because ESL Pull-Out programs will not necessarily satisfy the needs of all English Language Learners. Option D is incorrect because the use of technology will not necessarily satisfy the cultural needs of all students.
47	**10**	**B**	Option **B** is correct because the teacher informs parents about the purpose of a **Bilingual Program**. Option A is incorrect because a denial is not appropriate. Option C is incorrect because regular education is not an appropriate placement for the student. Option D is incorrect because the question does not focus on parents' English acquisition.
48	**10**	**C**	Option **C** is correct because the LPAC should address students' specific needs and review all pertinent information. Option A is incorrect because it is the LPAC committee responsibility to monitor a student who met exit criteria for the next two years. Option B is incorrect because the LPAC committee should first find the best instructional intervention for the student. Option D is incorrect because the student met exit criteria. The student's linguistic needs and oral proficiency are fine.
49	**10**	**B**	Option **B** is correct because it describes the primary duties of an **LPAC Committee**. Options A and C are incorrect because it is not the responsibility of the LPAC Committee to assess students' language proficiency. Option D is incorrect because it is not the LPAC's primary responsibility to classify students as English proficient only.
50	**10**	**B**	Option **B** is correct because it describes the membership of an LPAC Committee for bilingual programs based on the law. Option A is incorrect because a campus administrator is missing. Option C is incorrect because a parent representative is missing. Option D is incorrect because a campus administrator should be present.

USEFUL WEBSITES

www.quizlet.com
Create games, flash cards and study curriculum

http://www.ncela.gwu.edu
National Clearinghouse for English Language Acquisition

www.**usc**.edu/dept/education/CMMR/
Center for Multilingual Multicultural Research

http://lmrinet.gse.ucsb.edu
Linguistic Minority Research Institute

http://www.tea.state.tx.us/teks
Texas Education Agency

http://www.idra.org
Intercultural Development Research Association

http://www.cal.org
Center for Applied Linguistics

http://www.ed.gov/offices/OBEMLA/index.html
Office of Bilingual Education & Minority Language Affairs

http://www-rcf.usc.edu/~cmmr/crede.html
Center for Research on Education, Diversity & Excellence

http://www.tcbee.org/BilingualHomePage.htm
Division of Bilingual/ESL Programs/TEA

http://www.tabe.org
Texas Association of Bilingual Education

http://www.cal.org
Center for Applied Linguistics (CAL)

http://www.clmer.csulb.edu
Center for Language Minority Education & Research (CLMER)

http://www.crede.ucsc.edu
Center for Research on Education, Diversity & Excellence (CREDE)

http://www.duallanguagenm.org
Language of New Mexico – resources on program development, implementation and improvement, professional development and other resources

http://lmrinet.gse.ucsb.edu
Linguistic Minorities Research Institute (LMRI)

http://www.nabe.org
National Association for Bilingual Education (NABE)

http://www.ncela.gwu.edu
National Clearinghouse for English Language Acquisition (NCELA)

http://www.ed.gov/offices/OELA
Office of English Language Acquisition, Language Enhancement and Academic Achievement for Limited English Proficient Students (OELA)

ADITIONAL LINGUISTIC NOTES

PHONEME	**MORPHEME**	**LEXEME**	**LEXICON**
Smallest sound with meaning	Smallest unit with meaning	Word with different forms ruled by grammar	Dictionary words
/b/ boat /v/ vote /p/ pan /t/ tan	Book [book] free morpheme [s] bound morpheme (plural)	Run – runner/runs	Vocabulary words, Terms

	PRONUNCIATION	**SPELLING**	**MEANING**
HOMOPHONE *two/too* there/their for/four	**Same**	**Different**	**Different** Number/Also Direction/Possessive Preposition/Number
HOMOGRAPH desert/desert record/record minute/minute	**Different**	**Same**	**Different** *Arid region/leave* *Music storage/to tape/document* *Time/small*
HOMONYM mouth/mouth, left/left quarter/quarter	**Same**	**Same**	**Different** *Mouth of river, mouth of animal;* *Left direction, left leaving a place* *Time/Money*

KEY WORDS PER COMPETENCY AND PAGE NUMBER

CONTENT	COMPETENCY										
	1	2	3	4	5	6	7	8	9	10	Pg.
Language Concepts and Acquisition	X										12
Defining Language: Linguistic/Communicative competence, Grammar, Social Communicative competence, Grammatical competence, Discourse competence, Socio-linguistic competence, and Strategic competence.	X										13
Phonetics: Speaking, Point of Articulation, and Manner of Articulation, Stops, fricatives, glottal, affricates, nasals.	X										14, 15
Phonology: Phonemes, Allophones, Voiced Sounds, and Voiceless Sounds, Voicing, Minimal pairs.	X										16, 17
Suprasegmental Phonology: Length, Tone, Intonation, Stress, Syllable Structure - Onset and Rime. Prosody, Prosodic and Orthographic Stress.	X										18
Morphology: Morphemes, Allomorphs, Prefixes, Suffixes, Affixes, Infixes, Roots.	X										19
Lexicon: Lexemes, Free and Bound Morphemes.	X										19
Syntax: Phrases, Sentences, Word Order.	X										20
Semantics: Denotation, Connotation, Prosodic elements, Synonymy/Synonyms, Antonym/Antonyms, Polysemy, Homophony, idioms.	X										19, 20, 21
Pragmatics: Discourse, Discourse Analysis, Register.	X										21
Discourse: Rules of conversation, speech registers, Formal, Informal, Nonverbal communication.	X										21
Language Borrowing: Foreign words; rodeo, chocolate.	X										21
Language Interference: Interference, Intraference.	X										22
Code Switching: Interlanguage, Intersentential, Intrasentential.	X										22
Nouns: Singular, Plural, Non-Count, Count, Possessive, Collective.	X										23

CONTENT	COMPETENCY										
	1	2	3	4	5	6	7	8	9	10	Pg.
Pronouns, Articles, and Adjectives: Personal Pronouns, Indefinate and definate Articles, Comparative and Superlative Adjectives.	X										24, 25
Adverbs and Verbs: Regular and Irregular Verbs.	X										25, 26
Gerunds, and Objects: Direct Objects, Indirect Object.	X										26, 27
Present Progressive, Third Person Singular, and Voice: Active Voice, Passive Voice.	X										27
First Language Acquisition: Functions of a Language, Instrumental, Representational, Regulatory, Personal, Interactional, Heuristic, Imaginative, Informative.		X									30
Language Development: Babble, Holophrastic speech, and Telegraphic Speech.		X									30
Dialects: Standard Dialect, Lects, Sociolect, Genderlect, Regiolect, Idiolect, Accent, Slang, Jargon.		X									31
Behavioristic Approach: Repetition, Reinforcement, External Factors, Observation, Stimulus, Response.		X									32
Nativist Approach, overgeneralization: Innate, Cognitive, LAD.		X									32
Functional, Interactional, Cognitive Approaches: Cognitive Development, Language Development, Social Communication, Interaction, Language and Thought.		X									33
Second Language Acquisition		X									34
Individual Variables		X									34
Social Variables		X									34
Gardner's Socio-Educational Model		X									34
Lambert's Model		X									34
Stephen Krashen's Monitor Model: Acquisition Learning Hypothesis, Natural Order Hypothesis, Monitor Hypothesis, Input Hypothesis, and Affective Filter Hypothesis.											35, 36
Related Second Language Stages/Variables: Motivation, Silent Period/Preproduction, Anxiety, and Interest.		X									36

CONTENT	COMPETENCY										
	1	2	3	4	5	6	7	8	9	10	Pg.
Internalization of L2 Rules: Memorization, Categorization, Generalization, and Metacognition.		X									37
Separate Underlying Proficiency (SUP) Model, J. Cummins		X									38
Common Underlying Proficiency (CUP) Model. J. Cummins		X									38, 39
Threshold Theory, J. Cummins		X									40
Developmental Interdependence Hypothesis		X									41
Basic Interpersonal Communication Skills (BICS)		X									41
Cognitive/Academic Language Proficiency (CALP)		X									41, 42
Prism Model of Language Acquisition for School		X									42
Effective Practices, Resources, and Materials			X								43
Affective, Linguistic, Cognitive Support, realia, reading techniques, thinking aloud, L1 support.			X								45, 46
Grammar Translation Method			X								47
The Gouin and the Series Method			X								47
The Direct Method			X								47
The Audio-lingual Method (ALM)			X								47
The Cognitive Code Learning (Cognitive Approach)			X								47
Community Language Learning (CLL)			X								48
Suggestopedia			X								48
The Silent Way			X								48
The Total Physical Response			X								48
The Natural Approach			X								48
Notional-Functional Syllabus (NFS)			X								49
Content Based ESL, Pull-Out ESL			X								49
Self-Contained ESL Class, Cognitive and Academic Language Learning Approach (CALLA), Sheltered Instruction Observation Protocol (SIOP), Sheltered Instruction.			X								50
Technology Integration			X								51
English Language Proficiency Standards (ELPS)			X								51

CONTENT	COMPETENCY										
	1	2	3	4	5	6	7	8	9	10	Pg.
Linguistic/Communicative Competence				X							54
Four Linguistic Skills Acquired Interdependently				X							54
Oral Communicative Competence - Speaking and Listening, realia				X							54, 55, 56
Speaking - Proficiency Level Descriptors K-12 (Summary)				X							57
Individual and Social Factors Affecting Second Language Learning				X							58
Literacy Development					X						59, 60, 61
English Language Proficiency Standards (ELPS) Summary					X						62
Reading and Writing Proficiency Level Descriptors (K-1) Summary.					X						63
Reading and Writing - Proficiency Level Descriptors (2-12) Summary.					X						64
Early Stages of Reading: Phonological, Phonemic, and Graphophonemic Awareness, Fluency, Graphemes, Alphabetic Principle.					X						65
Literacy Research in Second Language Pedagogy: Graphophonemic, Semantic, Minimal Pairs.					X						66
Syntactic and Pragmatic					X						67
Literacy Methods/Approaches: Whole Approach, LEA Approach.					X						68, 69
Strategies for Reading Comprehension					X						69
Teaching Writing to English Language Learners: Factors affecting Literacy.					X						70, 71
Literacy and Biliteracy					X						72, 73
Content Area Instruction						X					75
Curriculum Requirements for ESL students						X					76, 77
Learning Strategies for English Language Learners						X					78
Metacognitive Strategies						X					78
Cognitive Strategies						X					78

CONTENT	COMPETENCY										
	1	2	3	4	5	6	7	8	9	10	Pg.
Social Affective Strategies: Motivation, Transfer, Prior Knowledge, Cognates, True and False Cognates.						X					79, 80
Examples of Graphic Organizers Across the Content Areas						X					81
Assessment Principles: Validity, Reliability, Cultural Bias.							X				84
Assessments: Summative, Formative.							X				85
Performance Assessment: Technology, Informal Observation, Portfolios, Peer Asessment, Anecdotal Logs, Conferencing, Norm-referenced Tests, Criterion-referenced Tests.							X				86
Assessments of Language Proficiency and Achievement of English Language Learners (ELLs)							X				86
Texas English Language Proficiency Assessment System (TELPAS)							X				87
State of Texas Assessment of Academic Readiness (STAAR)							X				87
Initial Identification Assessment and Annual Language Proficiency Monitoring - ELLs							X				88
Historical Background: The Naturalization Act of 1906.								X			91
Historical, Theoretical, and Policy Foundations: Colonial Era, Meyer v. State of Nebraska, Civil Rights Act, Bilingual Education Act, Lau v. Nichols, Castañeda v. Pichard, Plyler v. Doe, NCLB.								X			92-96
Instructional Program Models								X			97
Bilingual Education: Transitional early exit, Transitional Late exit.								X			98
Dual Language Programs: Two-Way, One-Way.								X			99
English as a Second Language (ESL): Content-based, pull-out.								X			100
Sheltered Instruction: Content and language. Modifications, Strategies, Comprehensible Input.								X			101
Self-Contained ESL Class								X			101
Cognitive and Academic Language Learning Approach (CALLA)								X			101

SEIDLITZ EDUCATION BOOK ORDER FORM

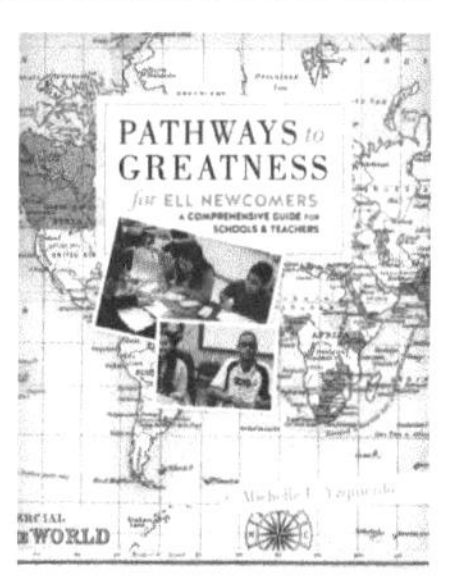

TITLE	PRICE	QTY	TOTAL$
NEW! 7 Steps To a Language-Rich, Interactive **Foreign Language** Classroom	$32.95		
NEW! Boosting Achievement: Reaching Students with Interrupted or Minimal Education	$26.95		
NEW! Motivating ELLs: 27 Activities to Inspire & Engage Students	$26.95		
NEW! Pathways to Greatness for ELL Newcomers: A Comprehensive Guide for Schools & Teachers	$32.95		
NEW! Sheltered Instruction in Texas: Second Language Acquisition Methods for Teachers of ELs	$29.95		
NEW! Talk Read Talk Write: A Practical Routine for Learning in All Content Areas K-12 2nd Edition	$32.95		
NEW! Teaching Social Studies to ELLs	$24.95		
NEW! Teaching Science to English Learners	$24.95		
NEW! ¡Toma la Palabra! SPANISH	$32.95		
NEW! Mi Cuarderno de Dictado SPANISH	$7.95		
7 Steps to a Language-Rich Interactive Classroom	$29.95		
38 Great Academic Language Builders	$24.95		
Diverse Learner Flip Book	$26.95		
ELPS Flip Book	$19.95		
COLUMN 1 TOTAL $			

TITLE	PRICE	QTY	TOTAL$
7 Pasos para crear un aula interactiva y rica en lenguaje SPANISH	$29.95		
ELLs in Texas: What Teachers Need to Know 2nd Edition	$34.95		
ELLs in Texas: What Administrators Need to Know 2nd Edition	$29.95		
Navigating the ELPS: Using the Standards to Improve Instruction for English Learners	$24.95		
Navigating the ELPS: Math 2nd Edition	$29.95		
Navigating the ELPS: Science	$29.95		
Navigating the ELPS: Social Studies	$29.95		
Navigating the ELPS: Language Arts and Reading	$34.95		
RTI for ELLs Fold-Out	$16.95		
Vocabulary Now! 44 Strategies All Teachers Can Use	$29.95		
Content Review & Practice for the TX ESL 154	$39.95		
Content Review & Practice for the TX Bilingual 164	$39.95		
Content Review & Practice for the TX Spanish 190	$39.95		
English/Spanish Linguistic and Academic Connections	$29.95		
Optimizando el desarrollo de la lectoescritura SPANISH	$39.95		
COLUMN 2 TOTAL $			

Pricing, specifications, and availability subject to change without notice.

COLUMN 1+2	$
DISCOUNT	$
SHIPPING	$
TAX	$
TOTAL	**$**

SHIPPING 9% of order total, minimum $14.95
5-7 business days to ship. If needed sooner please call for rates.
TAX EXEMPT? please fax a copy of your certificate along with order.

HOW TO ORDER

PHONE **(210) 315-7119** | ONLINE at **www.seidlitzeducation.com**
FAX completed form with payment info to **(949) 200-4384**

NAME

SHIPPING ADDRESS CITY STATE, ZIP

PHONE NUMBER EMAIL ADDRESS

TO ORDER BY FAX to **(949) 200-4384** please complete credit card info *or* attach purchase order

☐ Visa ☐ MasterCard ☐ Discover ☐ AMEX

CARD # EXPIRES *mm/yyyy*

SIGNATURE CVV *3- or 4- digit code*

☐ **Purchase Order attached**
please make P.O. out to **Seidlitz Education**

For information about Seidlitz Education products and professional development, please contact us at

(210) 315-7119 | kathy@johnseidlitz.com
56 Via Regalo, San Clemente, CA 92673
www.seidlitzeducation.com

Giving kids the gift of **academic language.**™

REV051120

SEIDLITZ PRODUCT ORDER FORM

Three ways to order

- **FAX** completed order form with payment information to **(949) 200-4384**
- **PHONE** order information to **(210) 315-7119**
- **ORDER ONLINE** at **www.seidlitzeducation.com**

Pricing, specifications, and availability subject to change without notice.

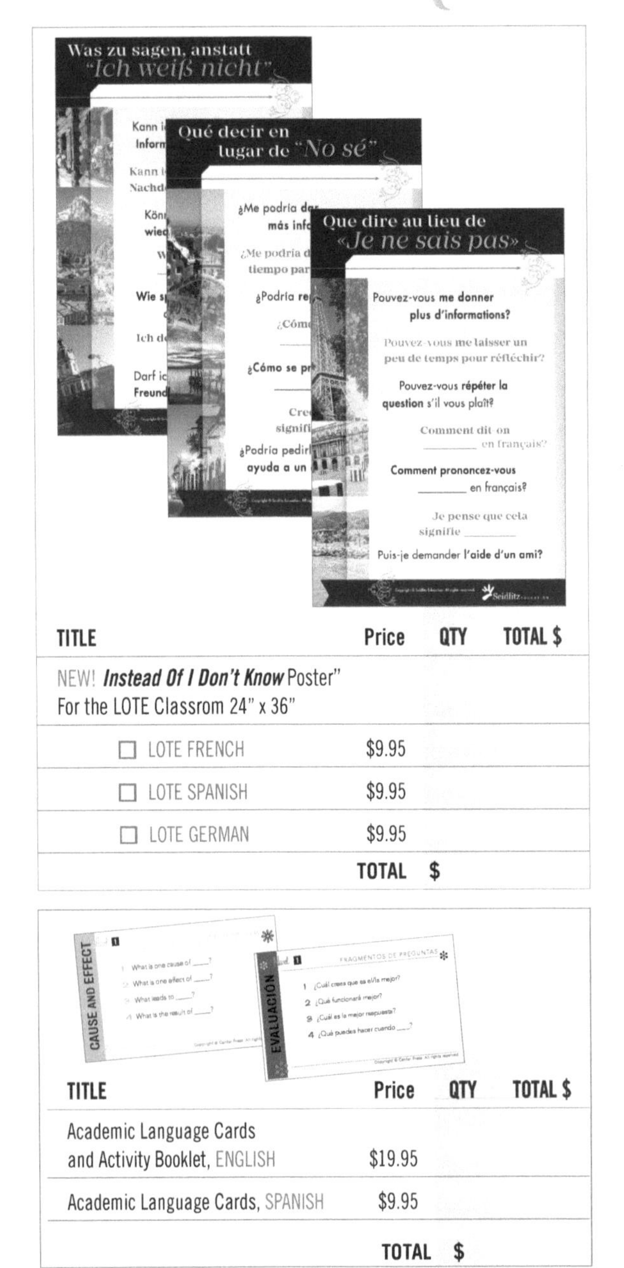

TITLE	Price	QTY	TOTAL $
NEW! ***Instead Of I Don't Know*** Poster" For the LOTE Classrom 24" x 36"			
☐ LOTE FRENCH	$9.95		
☐ LOTE SPANISH	$9.95		
☐ LOTE GERMAN	$9.95		
	TOTAL $		

TITLE	Price	QTY	TOTAL $
Academic Language Cards and Activity Booklet, ENGLISH	$19.95		
Academic Language Cards, SPANISH	$9.95		
	TOTAL $		

TITLE	Price	QTY	TOTAL $
Instead Of I Don't Know Poster, 24" x 36"			
☐ Elementary ENGLISH	$9.95		
☐ Secondary ENGLISH	$9.95		
20 pack ***Instead Of I Don't Know*** Posters, 11" x 17"			
☐ Elementary ENGLISH	$40.00		
☐ Secondary ENGLISH	$40.00		
Instead Of I Don't Know Poster, 24" x 36" Elementary SPANISH	$9.95		
20 pack ***Instead Of I Don't Know*** Posters, 11" x 17" Elementary SPANISH	$40.00		
	TOTAL $		

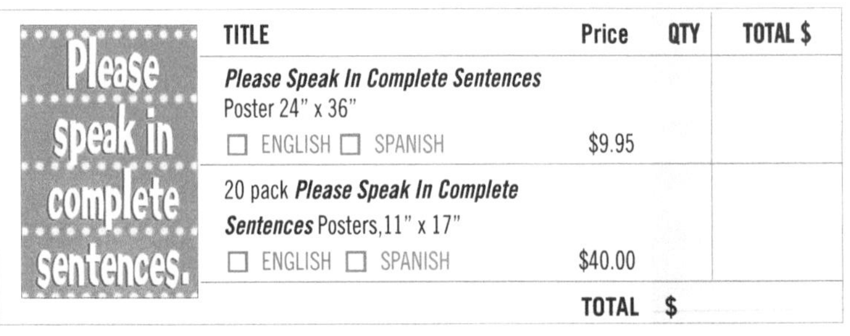

TITLE	Price	QTY	TOTAL $
Please Speak In Complete Sentences Poster 24" x 36" ☐ ENGLISH ☐ SPANISH	$9.95		
20 pack ***Please Speak In Complete Sentences*** Posters, 11" x 17" ☐ ENGLISH ☐ SPANISH	$40.00		
	TOTAL $		

SHIPPING 9% of order total, minimum $14.95
5-7 business days to ship.
If needed sooner please call for rates.

TAX EXEMPT? please fax a copy of your certificate along with order.

GRAND TOTAL	$
DISCOUNT	$
SHIPPING	$
TAX	$
FINAL TOTAL	$

NAME ____________________

SHIPPING ADDRESS ____________________ CITY ____________________ STATE, ZIP ____________________

PHONE NUMBER ____________________ EMAIL ADDRESS ____________________

TO ORDER BY FAX
to **(949) 200-4384**
please complete credit card info ***or*** attach purchase order

☐ **Visa** ☐ **MasterCard** ☐ **Discover** ☐ **AMEX**

CARD # ____________________ EXPIRES ____________ *mm/yyyy*

SIGNATURE ____________________ CVV ____________

☐ **Purchase Order attached**

please make P.O. out to **Seidlitz Education**